The Maya Apocalypse and Its Western Roots

The Maya Apocalypse and Its Western Roots

Matthew Restall and Amara Solari

ROWMAN & LITTLEFIELD
Lanham • Boulder • New York • London

Published by Rowman & Littlefield
An imprint of The Rowman & Littlefield Publishing Group, Inc.
4501 Forbes Boulevard, Suite 200, Lanham, Maryland 20706
www.rowman.com

86-90 Paul Street, London EC2A 4NE

Copyright © 2022 by The Rowman & Littlefield Publishing Group, Inc.

All rights reserved. No part of this book may be reproduced in any form or by any electronic or mechanical means, including information storage and retrieval systems, without written permission from the publisher, except by a reviewer who may quote passages in a review.

British Library Cataloguing in Publication Information Available

Library of Congress Cataloging-in-Publication Data
Names: Restall, Matthew, 1964– author. | Solari, Amara, 1978– author.
Title: The Maya apocalypse and its western roots / Matthew Restall and Amara Solari.
Description: Lanham : Rowman & Littlefield, [2022] | Includes bibliographical references and index.
Identifiers: LCCN 2021020912 (print) | LCCN 2021020913 (ebook) | ISBN 9781538154977 (cloth) | ISBN 9781538154984 (paperback) | ISBN 9781538154991 (epub)
Subjects: LCSH: Two thousand twelve, A.D. | Maya calendar. | Maya philosophy. | Prophecies. | End of the world. | Millennialism. | Civilization, Western. | Civilization, Medieval.
Classification: LCC F1435.3.C14 R472 2022 (print) | LCC F1435.3.C14 (ebook) | DDC 909/.09821—dc23
LC record available at https://lccn.loc.gov/2021020912
LC ebook record available at https://lccn.loc.gov/2021020913

To our Dads,
again, and always.

Contents

List of Figures ix
Introduction: You Really Can Survive 1

1 The History of the End of the World: The Maya Prediction 9
2 They Deserve Better: The Maya Evidence 29
3 God Is Angry: The Millenarian Mother Lode 49
4 The Moctezuma Factor: The End of the World Comes to Mexico 69
5 Apocalypto: The Millennium Comes to the Maya 91
6 We Are Always Almost There: Why People Believe 113

Sources and Suggestions for Further Reading 137
Index 145
About the Authors 153

Figures

I.1.	Dan Piraro, "I only had enough room to go up to 2012," *Bizarro* (comic strip).	3
I.2.	Dan Piraro, "Cheer up, pal. It's not the end of the world," *Bizarro* (comic strip).	4
1.1.	Monument 6 from El Tortuguero.	11
1.2.	Map of the Maya area.	14
1.3.	Stela 25, Izapa.	18
1.4.	Stela C (south side) at Quiriguá, carved in 775.	21
1.5.	Stela C (east side) at Quiriguá, carved in 775.	22
1.6.	*The Invocation of the Gods and the Grand Deluge*, from the Dresden Codex, pp. 73–74.	24
2.1.	*Left*, portion of Naranjo Altar 1: J5–J11; *right*, portion of new La Corona, Panel 2: V5–V8.	30
2.2.	The Temple of the Cross, Palenque.	35
2.3.	Ix Ahau Na (Lady House) from the Dresden Codex, p. 49.	37
2.4.	*The Mayan Empire*: A 2010 educational graphic from boston.com.	40
2.5.	Gaspar Antonio Chi, *The Mani Land Treaty Map*, 1557 (extant copy from 1600).	46
3.1.	Albrecht Dürer, *The Apocalyptic Woman*, 1511.	51
3.2.	Franz von Hauslab the Younger, *Daniel Interprets Nebuchadnezzar's Dream*, 1815–1853.	53

3.3.	Albrecht Dürer, *The Last Judgment*, from *The Small Passion*, 1509–1511.	57
3.4.	The Hellmouth, from the Winchester Psalter, twelfth century.	58
3.5.	Frontispiece to *Vaticinia, siue Prophetiae abbatis Ioachimi, et Anselmi episcopi Marsicani*; Venice: Hieronymum Porrum (and) Giovanni Battista Bertoni, 1589.	61
3.6.	Albrecht Dürer, *St. Francis Receiving the Stigmata*, 1503.	64
4.1.	Quetzalcoatl, from the Codex Telleriano-Remensis, folio 10r, sixteenth century.	71
4.2.	The New Fire Ceremony, from the Codex Borbonicus, p. 34, sixteenth century.	74
4.3.	The Calendar Stone, 1479.	76
4.4.	The open chapel of Actopan, Hidalgo, Mexico, sixteenth century.	84
4.5.	*The Maws of Hell* mural, from the open chapel of Actopan, Hidalgo, Mexico, sixteenth century.	85
4.6.	Moctezuma, from the Codex Durán, or *The History of the Indies of New Spain*,1581.	89
5.1.	Frederick Catherwood, *Ruins at Izamal*, from the book *Incidents of Travel in Yucatan*, 1843.	92
5.2.	The precontact pyramidal base of the monastic complex of Izamal, Yucatan, Mexico.	93
5.3.	The atrium of the monastic complex, Izamal, Yucatan, Mexico.	94
5.4.	North wall mural of the Izamal monastery *portería*, sixteenth century.	95
5.5.	South wall mural of the Izamal monastery *portería*, sixteenth century.	96
5.6.	East wall mural of the Izamal monastery *portería*, sixteenth century.	97
5.7.	Fernando Castro Pacheco, *Diego de Landa and the Mani Inquisition of 1562*, located in the Palacio de Gobierno, Merida, Yucatan, Mexico.	99

5.8.	Folio 49v from the *Books of the Chilam Balam of Chumayel*.	104
6.1.	Oliver Redding, "The End Is Nigh," cover for *The Official Magazine for the Apocalypse*, volume 3.	119
6.2.	New York City's apocalyptic end in *Amazing Stories*, January 1929.	121
6.3.	Frederick Catherwood, *Broken Idol at Copan*, from *Views of Ancient Monuments in Central America, Chiapas, and Yucatan*, London, 1844, tinted lithograph.	127
6.4.	Chicxulub, Yucatan, as ground zero for the dinosaur apocalypse.	130
6.5.	Promotional postcard for *2012*, Sony Pictures, 2009.	131
6.6.	*The Apocalypse*, from "The Abingdon Apocalypse," thirteenth century.	132
6.7.	Timo Essner, "The End Is Nigh," 2020.	134

Introduction

You Really Can Survive

The Apocalypse shall be the work of man, not of God.
—Homero Aridjis, "Discreation," 2012

We're gonna party like its 3012 tonight.
—Justin Bieber, "Beauty and a Beat," 2012

In the opening years of the twenty-first century, something extraordinary happened to Maya civilization. Ancient Maya knowledge became intensely relevant to millions of people worldwide, in ways that varied from the silly to the serious, from the controversial to the contested. A culture that had been unknown to much of the earth's six billion inhabitants at the turn of the century—or assumed by those who *had* heard of "the Mayans" to have vanished a millennium ago—was suddenly back. And it was back with an urgent message.

The notion that the world might soon be coming to an end began to spread about the same time—not coincidentally—that the Internet began to take off in the 1990s. Apocalyptic anxiety was hardly new, but it showed a particular vitality as the year 2000 (or Y2K, as it was commonly dubbed) and the new millennium approached. It was also increasingly driven by a new motor: the Maya connection and the specific claim that the ancient Maya had carefully calculated a very specific end date, one that was right around the corner. Websites like 2012-doomsday-predictions.com and chichen2012.org (now both defunct) began to proliferate, many with clocks counting down until the end. Dozens, then hundreds, of books came out on the 2012 phenomenon, warning us to prepare for the cataclysmic end or describing the wonderful new world to follow. Even the *Complete Idiot's Guide to 2012* took the whole thing more seriously than one might, in retrospect, imagine. Survival kits sold fast, urging online buyers to hurry while supplies—and the world—lasted.

As the first decade of the century advanced, there was an increasing proliferation of blog chatter and websites devoted to revealing how the ancient wisdom of Indigenous peoples could "show us our future." For some, that future was an apocalyptic end of time, prompting thousands of people to book their Doomsday vacations for the Grand Canyon, Stonehenge, Giza, Machu Picchu, or the Maya pyramids of Tikal and Chichén Itzá (figure 1.2 identifies the various Maya sites discussed in the book). An International Star Party series kicked off at Copán, with the third—billed as the final one—scheduled for 2012. The looming apocalypse had become sufficiently well-publicized and familiar for it to be lampooned by cartoonists (our favorites being by Dan Piraro; examples are figures I.1 and I.2).

For others, 2012 promised the dawn of a new era. The end of the world, it seemed, would not be all bad. One site warned that "2012 Is Real," with a countdown to the end; but not to worry, "you really can survive." John Major Jenkins (1964–2017), who had built a career on 2012 predictions, argued in dozens of books, essays, and interviews that the "end" was actually a beginning and a "new chance to recreate our world." On chichen2012.org, next to the link to learning "more about 2012," was a button to "Chichén Kids, upload your pics, participate and [have] fun" (and, by the way, "It's Free").

Either way, doom or new dawn, there was something unnerving about watching the clock tick down to zero. Because the increasingly apocalyptic atmosphere in which we lived in the years leading up to 2012 was hard to avoid, and end-of-the-world fever was easy to catch, reassurances that we "really can survive" were not to be taken lightly. Furthermore, somewhere at the heart of all this "2012ology" (to borrow Jenkins's invention) were the Maya, the creators of one of the most impressive and revered civilizations in human history. The ancient Mayas were not to be dismissed; maybe they had been on to something.

Perhaps the Maya understood that natural disasters and human blunders would always threaten to destroy our world. After all, didn't they themselves disappear (still a widely believed myth, despite protests by generations of Mayanists and the existence of millions of Mayas

Figure I.1. Dan Piraro, "I only had enough room to go up to 2012," *Bizarro* comic strip. (Reproduced with the kind permission of Dan Piraro.)

today)? Furthermore, in the few years before 2012, the news was full of horror stories about hurricanes, earthquakes, tsunamis, volcanoes, oil spills, global warming, nuclear stockpiles, and terrorist bombings. Even the 2012 Olympic Games, held in London, became a focus of conspiracist and apocalyptic expectations. Was it not possible that centuries of stargazing led Maya religious specialists to conclude that there was a pattern to the world's catastrophes? And, furthermore, that such a pattern

Figure I.2. Dan Piraro, "Cheer up, pal. It's not the end of the world," *Bizarro* comic strip. (Reproduced with the kind permission of Dan Piraro.)

might just culminate on the day 13.0.0.0.0 in the ancient Maya calendar that we call the "Long Count"—the day that was, in our calendar, December 21, 2012?

The fact that the world was still intact and turning on December 22, 2012, was only briefly reassuring. In the decade that followed, it often seemed as though the world *was* ending—not in a one-day cataclysm, but gradually—with each record-breaking extreme-weather event, each political upheaval, and each sign that the COVID-19 pandemic might just be our protracted end-time. Perhaps the Maya prophets were right after all. Speculation that the prediction was sound but the calendrical correlation was wrong, prompted parodies and memes—especially as December 21, *2021* approached (e.g., 2012 was an intern's typo)—but jokes have always fronted Doomsday distress. Perhaps, as some websites insisted, the problem was not the prophecy but the preoccupation with dates. As signs-of-end-times.com warned: "time is almost up"; "we are living right at the end of time"; "the end of time, as we know it, is **near**." How near, exactly? "We never set dates," the website proclaimed (although 2030 and 2050 were repeatedly mentioned on the site, as of 2021). "It is Satan who keeps setting these dates," false dates that, when they pass without the world ending, cause "many people to turn away completely from the truth."

That "truth"—that the end is imminent, and the need to face it is urgent—is the constant, common factor to all the time and attention given to the notion of the Apocalypse. For all the fixation on one date or another, the passing of a prophesied final day does little to quell apocalyptic anticipation (as we shall see). A few years after the world failed to end in 2012, two separate polls concluded that almost one-quarter of the British public believed the end would likely come *in their lifetime*. Americans were almost as fearful, while an average of 14 percent of people polled across twenty nations agreed with British end-times pessimists. Even in the twenty-first century, religion is frequently associated with end-times predictions—the prophets often being evangelical Christian, for reasons we shall explore in this book, but also Islamic and Jewish. And yet the anxious public has, for decades, ranked nuclear war and environmental catastrophe as the most likely causes of our proximate ending, with Judgement Day a distant third (or, in Britain, ranked equally with a zombie apocalypse). Low on the list, but always present, is the expectation of cataclysmic alien invasion.

The lack of a consensus on when and how the end will come is rooted in—and likewise nurtures—a fearful conviction that the answers are embedded in a secret knowledge. Elemental to the concept of secret knowledge is the belief that some cultures (or privileged people within them) *do* know the secret, and while some wish to keep it hidden, others seek to reveal and share it. The structure of that belief easily accommodates the triple notions of ancient knowledge (rendered secret by the passage of time), encoded knowledge (safeguarded until those in the know or those chosen can decode it), and conspiracy theories (explaining the persistence of the secret). That tripartite structure is ideally suited to the misappropriation of ancient Maya civilization.

We therefore begin our exploration of these phenomena with the Maya themselves; most 2012 Doomsday prophecies began with the Maya, and the passing of 2012 has not extinguished the popular notion that the Maya were predictors of the Apocalypse. As it turns out, the topic of our perennial apocalyptic obsession offers an effective avenue into exploring and understanding one of human history's most fascinating and misunderstood civilizations—albeit not in the way that one might at first imagine. Our first chapter identifies the relevant Maya texts and images and explains what they say and how they appeared to predict the world's demise. The second chapter then revisits and closely examines that evidence, as we analyze precisely what Maya priests and scribes did and did not prophesize. We offer a brief summary of Maya civilization, placing the topic of Maya prophecy in the larger context of who the Maya were and how they viewed their world.

In our third chapter, we step away from the Maya to look elsewhere for answers—and find them on the other side of the Atlantic Ocean. We argue that it is Western (largely Judeo-Christian)—not Maya—civilization that contains what we call the millenarian mother lode. While Maya culture flourished in the Classic period (roughly the eight hundred years after AD 250), civilization in the Mediterranean and Western Europe increasingly embraced millenarian ideas. *Millenarianism* is the belief that an impending transformation will dramatically change society. *Millennialism* expects such transformations to happen every thousand years. *Chiliasm* (from the Greek *chilia*, "a thousand") is the specifically Christian version of these beliefs, rooted in the biblical Book of Revelation and emphasizing the thousand-year idyll that Christ's return will bring; the destructive, end-of-world (or *eschatological*) manifestation of this transformation is often called the *Apocalypse*. Related terms will pop up later in the book. They are all, significantly, rooted in European—not Mayan—languages.

Concepts of millenarianism and apocalypse were deeply embedded within the cultures that were brought by Europeans to the Americas. Those ideas, first of all, reached Central Mexico, influencing the Aztecs and their neighbors in the early sixteenth century—a story we explore in our fourth chapter. Soon after, Spaniards invaded the kingdoms of the Maya, expanding the influence of European culture into cities and towns across Yucatan and Guatemala. In our fifth chapter, we explore how Christian notions of Doomsday and the Second Coming of Christ were easily appropriated, resulting in the cataclysmic narratives recorded by Maya scribes in the early colonial period. As the centuries passed, those narratives were viewed as an entirely Maya cultural phenomenon; in fact, they were expressions of Christian Maya culture. They are often misused as the basis for modern, popular interpretations of the ancient Maya worldview and its prophecies.

Millenarian ideas were not restricted to premodern times. As Western civilization expanded across the Atlantic and moved into the modern era, apocalyptic ideas flourished in Europe and North America. Doomsday predictions never disappeared but simply jumped from one supposed end-of-world date to the next. Apocalyptic anxiety is still very much with us, post-2012, because its origins and driving force have nothing to do with the Maya and everything to do with Western civilization and—increasingly—global civilization. In recent decades, no year has escaped prophesies of doom; regardless of when you are reading these words, you'll find online a prediction that the end is months, if not days, away.

In our sixth and final chapter, we outline how that larger phenomenon provided the context for the 2012 industry of tours, novels, guides, and books—including the book that we published in 2011, titled *2012 and the End of the World*, upon which this book is based. We summarize the apocalyptic thread (with the end-date bringing the world's destruction) and the New Age thread (a secular version of age-old millennialism, with the end-date being a utopian dawn), as well as fringe threads such as that of backup cataclysms. The chapter wraps up the evidence and arguments made in the preceding pages while also offering a brief summary of why the 2012 phenomenon acquired such traction; why, in human societies in general, there have been tendencies to embrace end-of-world predictions and fears; and why such apprehension not only persists but has been increasing for the last century or more. In other words, when 2012 failed to end the world, why did it not therefore bring an end to apocalyptic anxiety?

In the end, have we unlocked all these mysteries? Have we decoded the secrets contained within ancient Maya wisdom, or the cosmic code of planetary movements, or the wisdom of the first Franciscan friars to preach in the New World? Not quite; but we have sought to take seriously a potentially silly topic, to ponder it with purpose because it is taken—and mistaken—so seriously by so many people; and because the end-of-the-world phenomenon, before and after 2012, has well-evidenced and fascinating historical roots that tell us something about our own culture history (as well as about ancient Maya society).

Our original *End of the World* book was written to tie in with a class on the topic that we taught together at Pennsylvania State University in the fall of 2012. The course's goal was not simply to debunk 2012 myths or reassure undergraduates that the world would not end a few days after the semester did (and, therefore, there *was* a point to taking the final exam). Rather, the purpose of the class—and the original book—was to use 2012ology as a vehicle for combining the sources and methods of art history and history to explain the medieval, modern, and Maya contributions to apocalyptic thinking, and thereby to find a fascinating tool with which to explore both Maya and Western civilizations. That remains the guiding goal of this book.

A few weeks into that fall 2012 semester, the university's computer system spat out the date for our final exam. As coincidence had it (although a couple of the students were spooked enough to wonder if it really was coincidence), the date assigned was December 21. That Friday came, the world did not end, everybody showed up to the final, they all passed the class, and the following night we threw a party worthy of celebrating the dawn of the next 5,126 years. For, although this book aims in part to explain what the 2012 fuss was all about, it also seeks to reassure you that the thousands of years of history explored here do not suggest that the end is nigh. On the contrary, they show that, time and time again, we cannot help but fear that "final"—even as we begin to celebrate the new dawn.

• 1 •

The History of the End of the World

The Maya Prediction

> This is the history of the end of the world . . . the flood shall take place for the second time; this is the destruction of the world; this then is its end.
>
> —from the colonial-period Yucatec Maya Book of the Jaguar Prophet (*Books of Chilam Balam*)

> Predicted by the Mayans. Confirmed by science. Never before in history has a date been so significant to so many cultures, so many religions, scientists, and governments.
>
> —from the promotional material for Sony Pictures' *2012*

At a remote point along the road that runs between two large towns in the Mexican state of Tabasco, a large, concrete factory was built. The site was chosen for its access to stone and its location beside a highway. As far as anyone knew, or cared, nothing important lay there—no homes or valuable land. In the course of the factory's construction in the 1960s, a few man-made "hills" were bulldozed. By chance, several carved stone tablets were spotted among the rubble. They were saved, passed along to local officials, and eventually deposited in a Mexican museum as curiosities. The hieroglyphs could not be read, and no one could therefore be sure how old or how significant the stones might be.

In fact, the factory had been built upon an ancient Maya city, which was completely destroyed by the construction. Known to archaeologists today as El Tortuguero, the city was one of the most important smaller Maya sites in the region, aligned with—and tied dynastically through its rulers—to the impressive city of Palenque (in today's neighboring state of Chiapas). The heyday of El Tortuguero seems to have been the seventh century; most of the carved monuments rescued from the site date from the reign of Balam Ahau (Bahlam Ajaw in modern orthography, Jaguar Lord, r. AD 644–679). Probably related to the great Palenque ruler, K'inich Janaab' Pakal (to whom we shall return), Balam was a successful monarch in his own right, defeating nearby Comalcalco in 649, for example. He celebrated his twenty-fifth year on the throne by rebuilding a pyramid and temple put up by an ancestor in 510, dedicating it on January 11, 669. The building and its inscribed monuments survived thirteen centuries, until they were pulverized by bulldozers in the 1960s—all shattered, save for those stone fragments pulled from the wreckage.

The rescued monuments gathered dust for decades, until advances in Maya epigraphy (the decipherment of glyphs) inspired scholars to take a look at the long-forgotten, fragmented texts on the El Tortuguero stones. One of them was dubbed Monument 6 by Mayanists (Mayanists—the large international community of professional and amateur scholars who study the Maya, especially the ancient Maya, rather than their present-day descendants—give cities, buildings, and monuments names and numbers that tend to stick, even when the real names are later translated). Monument 6 had been broken up and its fragments scattered—four in a local Mexican museum, one in the Metropolitan Museum of Art in New York, two in private collections, and several other pieces lost. But when reconstructed, the glyphic text told not only the history of the ruler who had commissioned the monument but also seemed to have calendrical significance.

Despite the damage, scattering, and the loss of portions presumably destroyed by construction in the 1960s (if not before), Monument 6's glyphs are legible (illustrated in figure 1.1). There are various ways to transcribe alphabetically and translate such a text; that caveat aside, the text can be read as: *Tzuh tzahoom uyuxlahuun pikta / Chan ahau ux unii / Uhtooma ili / Yeni yen bolon yookte kuh / Ta chak hohoyha*. The literal meaning of this might be: "The thirteenth one will end on 4 Ahau, the third of Uniiw. There will occur blackness and the descent of the Bolon Yookte' god to the red." Alternatively, the second line might read: "There will occur a seeing, the display of the god Bolon Yookte' in a great investiture." A more idiomatic translation would read something like this: "The thirteenth calendrical cycle will end on the day 4 Ahau,

Figure 1.1. Monument 6 from El Tortuguero. (Drawing by David Stuart.)

the third of Uniiw, when there will occur blackness (or a spectacle) and the God of the Nine will come down to the red (or be displayed in a great investiture)."

The meaning is hardly clear, but with the application of some imagination the text can become an ominous warning, perhaps even an apocalyptic one. It certainly became one of the sparks—by some accounts, *the* spark—that ignited the firestorm of the 2012 phenomenon. The Tortuguero text was cited over and over, starting in 1996 (when epigraphers Stephen Houston and David Stuart first published a translation of it), as the earliest example of Maya predictions of the world's end. This was partly because scholars initially speculated that the text might be a rare case of Classic Maya prophecy; subsequent retractions (to which we shall turn in the next chapter) fell on deaf ears. It was also partly because the passage's enigmatic and incomplete nature invites speculation: if we choose the first translation variant, black and red, the colors of darkness and blood, seem portentous; who is this god called Bolon Yookte', or the nine Yookte' gods, or the Gods of the Nine, and what catastrophe might his or their descent to Earth herald?

Above all, the Tortuguero passage sparked controversy because the date to which it refers fell in our own lifetimes; in our calendar, it is December 21, 2012 (sometimes given as 10 or 23, but usually 21, the winter solstice). In the Maya calendar, the date is a series of glyphs representing numbers; written out using our numbers, that date is 13.0.0.0.0. The zeros seem ominous, and the cycle whose end it marks is impressively long: 5,126 years (more specifically, 1,872,000 days or 5,126.37 years). That span of time takes us back to the dawn of human cultural complexity—the beginnings of dynastic Egypt, the rise of Minoan civilization, the inception of Stonehenge, and, perhaps too, the dawn of the Maya world. Had the Maya calculated that settled human life existed within a specific time frame, a kind of cosmic, civilizational clock? And if so, is the tick of that clock getting louder and louder? Is the alarm about to go off?

∼

It is tempting to comb through Maya literature to find clues as to what the Maya thought would happen on the day 13.0.0.0.0, and indeed many succumbed to that temptation. Before we turn to look at some of those clues—in Maya carvings, ancient glyphs, and colonial-period alphabetic texts—a brief explanation of four core aspects of Maya civilization is necessary. These are political organization in the Maya region: the nature of Maya religion; the structure of the calendar; and creation mythology.

The Maya area was never politically unified. The peoples that we call "the Maya" comprised a culture group or civilization; they all shared a discrete set of cultural traits. But, although they spoke dialects of the same family (the Mayan language family), all the Maya never spoke the same language. Nor did they ever recognize a common sense of identity or answer to a single ruler or dynasty. The region, stretching today from southern Mexico across Guatemala and Belize into Honduras, contained hundreds of polities (see figure 1.2). For thousands of years leading up to the Spanish invasion that began in the 1520s, small Maya kingdoms vied for regional control. Some built spectacular cities and conquered their neighbors. But no kingdom was able to dominate the whole Maya area, let alone any of its most populated and prosperous regions—such as northern Yucatan or lowland Guatemala.

Maya rulers were kings, meaning that they held the top spot of an extremely steep social hierarchy. The position was seen as granted by the deities, a divine authority legitimated through familial bloodlines and religious abilities. The king was a *kul ahau* (pronounced "koo-hool a-HOW," or *k'uhul ajaw*), a "sacred ruler." During the seven centuries that archaeologists call the Classic period (third to tenth centuries AD), most of these sacred kings were seen as genetically related to the deities who had created the universe, and from them traced their lineage. Politics and religion were intertwined; an entire social class was devoted to religion—a priestly class, whose members were often close family members of the ruler or from other elite families. The religion they oversaw was complex and variable, composed of an elaborate pantheon of sacred beings, including both gods and deified ancestors.

The Maya pantheon was supported by a well-developed ritual tradition, based upon the concept of reciprocity. Various mythistories maintained that, in the primordial past, deities had sacrificed themselves to establish the cosmos; in some cases, godly bodies were refashioned to create celestial bodies, the flesh of human beings, and even the material matrices of the earth—the water, vegetation, and so forth. Humans responded by performing rituals as a form of debt payment; that is,

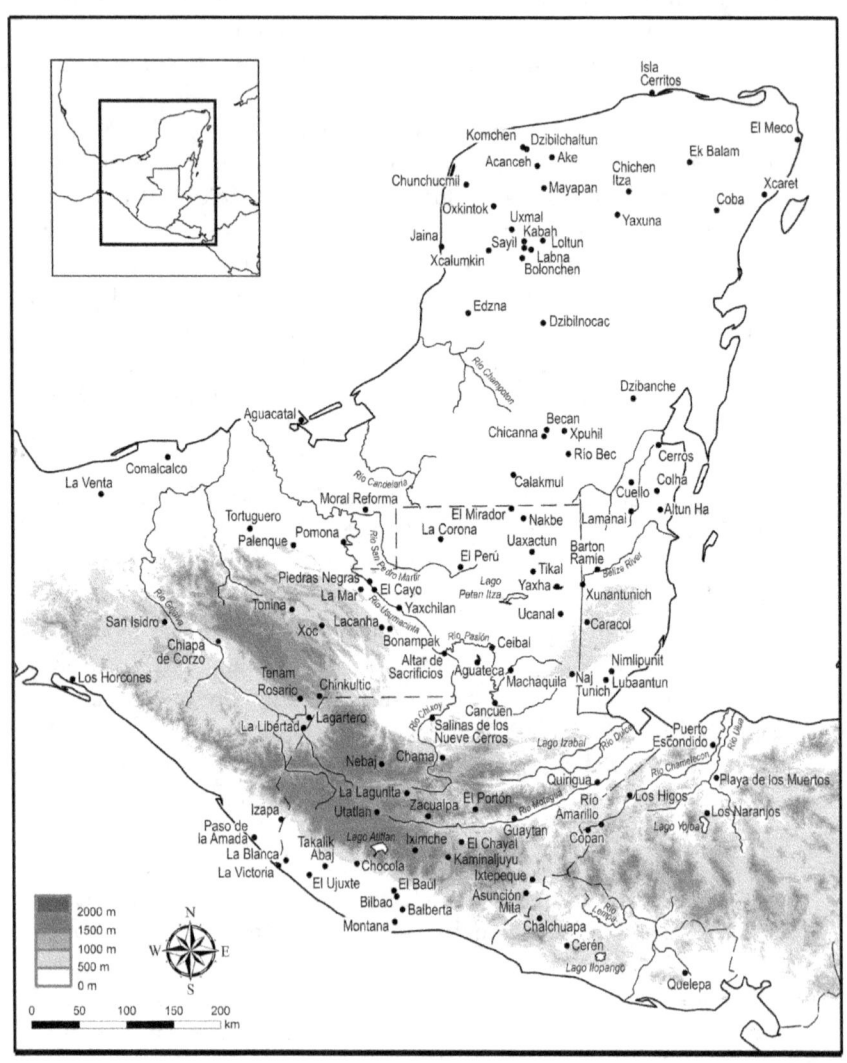

Figure 1.2. Map of the Maya area. (Reproduced with the kind permission of Stephen D. Houston and Takeshi Inomata, from *The Classic Maya*, Cambridge University Press, 2009, p. 4.)

proscribed veneration was performed as the primary means of keeping the deities sustained and, thus, the cosmos in order. A cosmos in balance was necessary for human survivability. Only the correct amount of rain, predictable seasons, and the avoidance of pests (all controlled by the deities) would ensure a robust harvest, thus avoiding famine and disease.

Maya gods had humanlike personalities—social biographies, if you like—and engaged in their own forms of revelry and collective drama. In keeping with the regional nature of Maya identity, these deities were frequently localized; even when peoples from different ends of the Maya area worshiped the same deity, each viewed the deity as their own and claimed it had originated or been "born" in their home cities. In fact, some monumental temples proclaimed that specific deities had been birthed within them, with inscriptions—some surviving to this day—naming these structures "sweatbaths," the traditional location for childbirth to take place in the Maya world.

Maya calendrics is a complex topic, and a great deal has been written on it; what follows is a crude simplification. To the best of our knowledge, the Maya and their neighbors in southern Mexico developed solar (365-day) and lunar/gestational (260-day) calendars three to four thousand years ago. These were cyclical counts, similar to our solar calendar (of 365-day years) and lunar calendar (our months). Probably around the second or third century BC, a further calendar was developed, which Mayanists call the Long Count. This calendar, as its name suggests, views the passing of the years on a larger scale, longitudinally. The Long Count did not begin in the third century but was dated back to an earlier starting point—in our calendar, August 14, 3114 BC—and from then stretched forward in time for 5,126 years (it is highly unlikely that the Long Count was created close to its start date, as that predated the emergence of Maya society by many centuries).

The Long Count cycle was composed of multiple minicycles, the shortest being a single day (the *k'in*, also the word for "sun," roughly pronounced "keen"). The Maya counting system was vigesimal (a base of twenty, as opposed to our base of ten), so the next cycle was composed of twenty days (the *winal*, or *uinal*, pronounced "WEE-nal"); eighteen of these *winal* composed yet another cycle (the *tun*, pronounced like a short "toon"; in Yucatec Mayan, *tun* also means "stone"). The *tun* totaled 360 days and approximated the solar year. Expanding further, twenty *tun* created the *k'atun* (7,200 days, about twenty years) and twenty *k'atun* created the four-hundred-year *b'aktun* (specifically, 144,000 days). The calendar had the potential to expand infinitely; one cycle, called the *alawtun*, comprised twenty-three million days. As we shall see in a moment, some Maya cities advertised their mathematical skills by carving stone sculptures with Long Count dates reaching into billions of years. Mayanists write out the Long Count as a series of numbers, separated by periods and running from right to left (the Maya themselves tended to write them in paired columns). For example, a date of 1 day, 12 *winal*, 3 *tun*, and 2 *k'atun* would be written as 2.3.12.1.

One interpretation of the Long Count argues that it is by its very nature "predictive." According to this theory, the Long Count was not created by selecting a starting date and then counting forward, the way we count from our Gregorian calendar year, zero (which supposedly marks the birth of Jesus Christ) forward to 2012. Instead, the theory goes, the Maya selected a significant end date and then counted backward. The ancient Maya determined that end date by calculating when, in the future, the various cycles of the calendar would coincide on a winter solstice day. Such a method would privilege December 21, 2012, making it, in a sense, the *key date* within the entire complex edifice of Maya calendrics. We are not persuaded by this theory; there are other ways of interpreting the Long Count calendar—and we shall turn to them in the next chapter. But for now, we leave you with the possibility that the Maya built their Long Count calendar specifically so they could know when its final day—perhaps *the* final day—would fall.

The final aspect of Maya civilization that needs to be briefly explained here is creation mythology. Our understanding of this mythology is based on two kinds of sources. One is ancient sources—glyphic texts and images in stone sculptures, painted ceramics, and codices, mostly created in the thousand years before European contact in the 1520s. The other source comprises texts written alphabetically in Mayan languages during the three centuries of colonial rule that followed that invasion—most importantly a K'iche' Mayan book called the *Popol Vuh* and a set of documents composed in Yucatec Mayan called the *Books of Chilam Balam* (both of which we shall examine in some detail below and also in chapter 5). This may seem like a large body of evidence, but it covers variations across the Maya area and over thousands of years. So, again, simplification is in order.

The core idea that is relevant here is the Maya belief that the world was created repeatedly. Previous creations by the gods were not successful (because, for example, humans made of wood were not capable of worshiping their creators) and were therefore destroyed. The dominant metaphor of global destruction was a great flood (hardly unique to the Maya; flood mythology can be found in almost every ancient culture throughout the world). Conflict between the gods of the sky and the gods of the underworld also played a role in these destructions. The current creation is the third or fourth and is the age of maize (corn)— humans were made from maize, the crop that therefore sustains us.

From a certain perspective, in the contexts of the Long Count and creation mythology, the Tortuguero monument could be read as predicting that December 21, 2012, would be a milestone day, the day that would mark the end of a great temporal cycle and would be accompanied by the next destruction of the world.

And indeed, some have argued that other ancient sites seem to support this impression. One example is the ancient city of Izapa. The largest ancient city in what is today the Mexican state of Chiapas, Izapa's heyday was the half-millennium from 600 to 100 BC. More than two hundred stela, altars, and other carved stone monuments have been found at the site. Although it is not technically a Maya city, and it lacks Long Count dates or any real glyphs at all, its monuments have been read as containing some of the earliest examples of calendrics and illustrations of Maya mythology. The dean of the spiritualist branch of 2012 predictions, John Major Jenkins, claimed that Izapa's monuments allow us to decode "the secrets of Mayan sacred science"; the site is "the origin place of the 2012 calendar and the 2012 prophecy."

Jenkins argued that one set of buildings (the structures that archaeologists call the Group F Ballcourt) are aligned to the sunrise and sunset of the solstices; that the structures display galactic creation imagery (such as a solar deity paddling down the Milky Way in a canoe); and that Stela 25 encodes a cosmic map. The image on the stela (figure 1.3) shows a man holding a staff with a bird perched at the top. Several Mayanists have interpreted the bird as representing the Big Dipper. Others suggest that the figure is one of the Hero Twins, who in Maya creation mythology shoots a bird deity named Seven Macaw out of a tree with a blowgun (the anecdote is recorded in later Maya sources, on the Classic-period "Blowgunner Pot" and in the great K'iche' Mayan manuscript

Figure 1.3. Stela 25, Izapa. (Drawing by the authors.)

called the *Popol Vuh*). According to the story, the Hero Twins had to shoot the macaw—also called the Principal Bird Deity by scholars—as penance for his narcissistic behavior.

There is also a caiman in the picture, who is bound head-down. Jenkins saw the caiman's head as the head of the Milky Way; the "nuclear bulge" of the galactic center is just below his eye. The dots on the caiman's back are the stars of the Milky Way. The Polar Center is at the top, with Seven Macaw (the Big Dipper) and the caiman aligned so as to represent the stars of the Milky War as they appeared over Izapa at midnight on the summer solstice when the stela was erected (around the start of the third century BC). The result of all the Izapa evidence, claimed Jenkins, is "a dateless reference to an astronomical scenario" that points to the moments of creation, both at "era-3114 BC" and at "era-2012." We shall return to Izapa in the next chapter.

Another example of a monument that was purported to have 2012 implications is Stela 63 in Copán, a spectacular Classic-period Maya city in what is now Honduras. The stela highlights the day 9.0.0.0.0 as a calendrical milestone. That day is in the year AD 435, not 2012, in our calendar. But the implication is that if 9.0.0.0.0 matters, then 13.0.0.0.0 will matter as much, if not more. This is equivalent to commemorating Y1K in our calendar, thereby lending significance to Y2K.

A similar example are the monuments in Cobá, a site in northeast Yucatan, which contain the oldest and largest dates recorded by the Maya. Cobá's Stela 1 (carved in AD 672) does not limit the year count to five temporal cycles (13.0.0.0.0 is a five-temporal cycle count). The Maya scribe counted back twenty-four places to carve a date that consists of twenty thirteens and four zeros. That is a date about a billion years longer than 13.7 billion BC, which is the age that astrophysicists currently assign to the universe. There's even more: by computing all the numerical periods on Stela 1 and Stela 5 (a companion monument carved ten years earlier), we reach a date—calculated in days, no less—that stretches twenty-eight octillion years (an octillion has twenty-seven zeros) *before* the 3114 BC start of the Long Count. That computation of days stretched even further into the future. In other words, the Long Count calendar was merely an abbreviation of a reckoning of time that was far vaster, one that David Stuart calls the Grand Long Count, encompassing "nearly seventy-two octillion years from beginning to end." Not only was 2012, therefore, not the end date but it wasn't even close to the middle.

The astronomical dates on Cobá's stelae may have merely been acts of "computational virtuosity" (as Mayanist Prudence Rice puts it), an exercise in showing off what could be done with the mathematics of the Long Count and Grand Long Count. Or the Maya elite at Cobá may have been demonstrating how the calendar was the formula that could be used to decode time, its numerical logic revealing when the universe was created and when each successive creation of the world and its humans occurred—and would occur. Either way, as Stuart has eloquently put it:

> The deep time of the full Maya calendar is stunning in its scale and in the virtuosity displayed by its internal mechanisms. I think it's fair to say that it constituted the grandest expression of time ever put down on stone or paper by any human mind. It certainly dwarfs our own understanding of the vast temporal scale of the universe.

It is worth, then, briefly taking in a couple more examples. One is an exquisite stone carving at Quiriguá, known as Stela C (see figures 1.4 and 1.5). The large hieroglyphs on the surface of Stela C clearly feature the date 13.0.0.0.0. Quiriguá, in southeast Guatemala, was a midsized Maya city that was occupied for about a thousand years (from roughly 200 to 1200). Its history was intertwined with that of nearby Copán, to which it was subject until a successful revolt in 738. The kings of Quiriguá commissioned an impressive number of stone sculptures of various kinds, including the tallest stone monuments, or stelae, in the Americas. Some of the most important of these were carved under the rule of Cauac Sky (more accurately, K'ak' Tiliw Chan Yoaat).

King from 724 to 785, it was Cauac Sky who attacked Copán, captured its ruler, and had him executed in Quiriguá's main plaza. It was also under Cauac Sky, in 775, when Stela C was erected. Its purpose was to commemorate and promote the divinity and legitimacy of the king by linking his reign to the creation of the cosmos. On the south side of the stela, the king himself appears in full war regalia, wearing a military headdress and anklets (figure 1.4).

The stela's opposite side (the north side) was carved to represent an anthropomorphic being, some kind of composite elderly human-tree creature, which anthropologist Matthew Looper suggests is symbolic of his divine patronage of one of the cycles of the 365-day calendar. The deity raises one foot as if in dance, while the Principal Bird Deity

Figure 1.4. Stela C (south side) at Quiriguá, carved in 775. (Photograph courtesy of the Harvard University Peabody Museum of Archaeology and Ethnology, 977-57-00/1.32.)

Figure 1.5. Stela C (east side) at Quiriguá, carved in 775. (Drawing by Matthew Looper, reproduced with his kind permission.)

perches above his head and umbilical cords flow to create the pattern of the universe. The west side is a long, hieroglyphic inscription that refers to a dedication ceremony made by an earlier king in 455 (we know this was not the first king, but Cauac Sky may have claimed him as a dynastic founder).

Finally, the east side of the stela, the most important for our story, relates the Maya mythological tale of the most recent creation, recording it as taking place in 13.0.0.0.0—not the future such date but the past one, the zero date of the Long Count, 3114 BC. Either seen in their surviving state as stone carvings or drawn (figure 1.5), the glyphs that inscribe this date exemplify the combined impact of Maya art and calendrics. The conjunction of creativity and knowledge, beauty and intellect, compel us to see meaning in this so-called Creation Text. "The tripod is revealed, three stones are bundled, they place a stone, Jaguar Paddler, Stingray Paddler," reads the text, following the lengthy recording of the date.

> It happened at First Five Sky, Jaguar Throne Stone, he plants a stone, [unnamed god], it happened at [unnamed city], Snake Throne Stone, and then it happened, he bundled a stone . . .

Continuing in this vein, the Quiriguá glyphs use the metaphor of the three hearth stones traditionally placed in Maya homes to describe the creation of the world. By referencing them as *throne* stones instead, Cauac Sky is also telling his subjects that his kingship is rooted in that same moment of creation—all the way back in 13.0.0.0.0 (3114 BC).

Cauac Sky's kingly ego was impressive, indeed; in one stone monument, he tied his rule to the creation of the universe, the creation of the world, and the origins of the city's divine dynasty. So how does this relate to the end of the world? Arguably, by linking his reign to creation, Cauac Sky also evokes destruction, the absence of the world before its creation, and the future possibility of such cycles of destruction and creation. Arguably.

What did the Maya think had happened at the moment of world destruction and re-creation? One possible answer is found on the final page of one of the few surviving Maya codices. The Dresden Codex, a bark-paper book created by a group of highly skilled Maya scribes in the fourteenth century, details the movements of the moon and planets and the resulting calendrical cycles. These all appear to

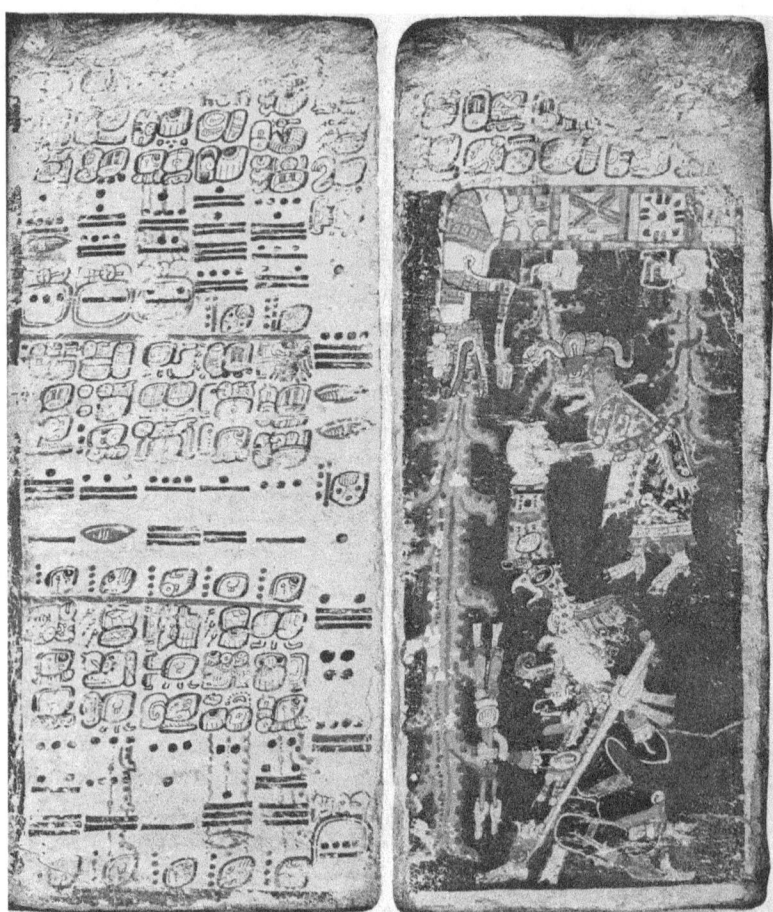

Figure 1.6. *The Invocation of the Gods and the Grand Deluge*, from the Dresden Codex, pp. 73–74. (Held by the *Sächsische Landesbibliothek*, Dresden; image in the public domain.)

culminate with a large caiman vomiting water from the sky (see figure 1.6). The image is a disturbing one, seeming to illustrate the destruction of the world in a great flood. Three great channels of water spew from the caiman. The glyphic text refers to the old goddess Chac Chel, who is pouring water from a jar in the center of the painting. The god Chac, painted black, crouches menacingly below, wielding weapons of destruction.

An apocalyptic interpretation of this final page of the Dresden Codex is especially compelling because the legend of the Great Deluge or the Flood appears elsewhere in Maya sources—indeed, in other parts of Mesoamerica (the larger civilizational area of which Maya civilization was a part). In Aztec creation mythology, for example, the fourth and most recent destruction and re-creation of the world took the form of the Flood. This is also how the current world is created in the K'iche' Maya narrative in the *Popol Vuh*; the humans made of wood are all swept away by the gods in the Flood. As Diego de Landa, a Franciscan friar in sixteenth-century Yucatan, was told by local Maya: previously *el mundo fue destruido por el diluvio*, "the world was destroyed by the Flood."

In the *Books of Chilam Balam* (Books of the Jaguar Prophet), that set of texts written in alphabetic Mayan in colonial-period Yucatan, the Flood is brought on by a battle between deities. The two main protagonists were the God of the Thirteen (Oxlahuntiku, god of the sky, which had thirteen levels), and the God of the Nine (Bolontiku, god of the underworld, which had nine levels). At one time, scores of towns and villages across Yucatan surely maintained their own version of these books—which contained a mixture of history and mythology, prophecy and calendrics, herbal lore and medicinal remedies—although less than a dozen survive today. The surviving manuscripts date from the late eighteenth century but contain material copied repeatedly from previous centuries, some of it likely transferred from glyphic books (codices) painted before the arrival of alphabetic writing and Christianity.

The books from Chumayel, Tizimin, and Mani feature almost identical versions of the creation myth that includes the Flood story. It is *u kahlay cab tu kinil*, "the history of the world in those days," declares the Chumayel version, which goes on to describe the epic battle between Oxlahuntiku and Bolontiku. After Oxlahuntiku wins,

> there was one rush of rain, one sharp burst of rain, as when the Archangel of the corn field came. The sky was stormy; it was stormy on earth too. The four gods spoke/stood, the four *bacabob* [rain gods], causing this destruction. Then when the destruction of the earth was finished, it [the earth] was settled, so that Kan Xib Yui [a bird god] can put it in order, and the white *imix* [ceiba] tree speak/stand to the north. It speaks/stands there as a pillar of the sky and also as a sign of the destruction of the world; this white ceiba tree speaks/stands in support. Then the black ceiba tree spoke/stood too,

where the black-bellied *pidzoy* [bird] lives. Then the yellow ceiba tree spoke/stood too, a sign of the destruction of the world; there the yellow-bellied *pidzoy* lives, and there sits Kan Xib Yui and the yellow *oyal mut* [bird]. Then the blue-green ceiba tree spoke/stood too, in the center. It sits, placed there, as a record of the destruction of the world.

What is going on here? Is this a Maya description of Doomsday? In a way, it is, albeit a veiled one. The passage uses creation mythology and the annual coming of the rains as metaphors for each other; a violent spring storm is like the Flood, destroying the world, but also leads to its re-creation as symbolized by trees and birds. The trees both speak and stand (the scribe uses *ual*, which is both *u al*, "it speaks," and *ual*, "to set up, stand"). They speak in testimony, as "signs" or symbols, of the world's "destruction," and they stand as pillars supporting the sky and thus maintaining the world from another destruction. These myth-trees, color-coded and oriented to the cardinal directions, are like Maya stelae—planted deep in the soil, they both stand and speak of the history of the (local) world.

The trees are called *imix che* for a reason. The term is a way of referring to a ceiba tree, which was symbolic and significant to the Maya in a similar way to how we see the oak tree. But there is a further reason: The Flood occurs at the end of the *k'atun*, or twenty-year cycle named *13 Ahau* and, in the calendar, the day following *ahau* is named *imix*. The trees are, thus, more than symbols of the world's destruction; they are named for the day after. They are, in the end, more about *The Day after Tomorrow* than about *2012*.

However, it may be read that the *Chilam Balam* text seems to be a different version of the Flood story, which is visually presented at the end of the Dresden Codex. But what of the caiman whose role is so vivid in the codex? Sure enough, in the version of the book from the towns of Mani and Tizimin, the caiman does make an appearance. This caiman, called Itzam Cab Ain, Lizard Earth Caiman, is not in the sky (as in the Dresden Codex image) but holds up the earth; and he does not spew water (as in the Dresden) but must be slain for the destructive flood to be complete:

> Then Itzam Cab Ain is born. The day is cut at dawn, so that the sky is split and the land revealed. And thus begins the book of Oxlahuntiku. Then a great flooding of the earth takes place; then up rises

the great Itzam Cab Ain; the end of the telling, the composition of the *k'atun*; that flood will be the end of the telling of the *k'atun*. But Bolontiku did not wish it. So he cut the throat of Itzam Cab Ain, who carries the land on his back.

In another passage, the caiman is absent; but the Flood seems to accompany an apocalyptic ending to the *k'atun* cycle:

> Here is when it shall end, the telling of the *k'atun*; that is what is given by God; the flood shall take place for the second time; this is the destruction of the world; this then is its end.

This brings us back to Tortuguero, and the connection is potentially ominous. "There will occur black . . . ," predict the glyphs on Monument 6; the weapon-wielding Chac in the Dresden image is painted black. The Tortuguero text seems to continue, "The Gods of the Nine will descend to the red . . ."; a manifestation of this god heralds the destruction of the world in the Flood, according to the *Chilam Balam* narratives. Named Bolon Yookte' K'uh (or Bolonyooktiku in colonial-period orthography) in the Tortuguero glyphs, he is Bolontiku in the *Chilam Balam* texts. The name is the same: *bolon* is "nine" and *ku* is "god"; the syllables in-between are, loosely speaking, locatives, with *yook* indicating a plurality. Bolontiku is the God of the Nine, the god of the nine levels of the underworld, and his presence in 2012, or so this logic tells us, is surely not a good sign.

One translator of the *Chilam Balam* literature, the late Munro Edmonson, has argued that some of the passages we have quoted above are from a celebration of the cycle that ended in 1618, a *Ceremonial of the Baktun* that took place in the Yucatec capital city of Merida. In the words of Edmonson and his Mayanist colleague Victoria Bricker, "This extravaganza was in honor of the fact that the date marked the beginning of an even *baktun*: 12.0.0.0.0." Of the twenty separate ceremonies, or what these scholars dub "acts of the drama," the third is the "cycle-ending ceremony." This features the battle described above, in which the God of the Nine defeats and sacrifices the God of the Thirteen; the image of the deity of the underworld rising up and slaughtering the deity of the heavens has clearly apocalyptic overtones.

According to Edmonson's reading, the ritual featured the following: "The millennial words here / For the examination / Of the Mayan people here / Who may know / How they were born / And settled the land / Here / In this country." For Edmonson, the passage reflected the fact that "competent hieroglyphic writing probably lasted" into the seventeenth century, "and the Long Count calendar certainly did." Here, then, were the Maya seeming to use formal "millennial" speech and ritual to mark the moment when the last *baktun* of four hundred years ended and the next one began? What was that next *baktun*? It was the one that ended in December 2012.

∽

Lay hay cabile lay tun cu dzocole: "This is the destruction of the world; this then is its end." The meaning of such a phrase seems clear; indeed, all these Maya texts and images seem to add up to something significant. Dates carved in stone monuments, images of apocalypse, narratives of cyclical catastrophe, all appear to support the notion that the Maya knew that the end was nigh—and they had figured out exactly when it would happen. Even so, without the Tortuguero monument and its specific citing of the winter solstice day in 13.0.0.0.0, 2012ology and the whole phenomenon might not have developed. Had one of those bulldozers in the 1960s moved a few feet one way or the other, we might have missed the warning.

· 2 ·

They Deserve Better

The Maya Evidence

> The Mayans [sic], who were good-enough astronomers and timekeepers to predict Venus's position 500 years in the future, deserve better than this.
>
> —*New York Times*, November 16, 2009

> 2012 has gained the status of an icon, a cultural symbol, to be used and often abused for purposes that have nothing to do with its origins and the intentions of its creators.
>
> —John Major Jenkins, *The 2012 Story*, 2009

Did the Maya try to warn us that the end was nigh?

To answer this question, we should begin where the first chapter began: with Monument 6 from El Tortuguero. Does that text tell us that the world will end "when the thirteenth cycle ends," that the Apocalypse will come when "the God of the Nine comes down to the red"?

In fact, the Tortuguero monument tells us no such thing. Its uniqueness and importance lie in the fact that it cites the date at the end of the Long Count. But ironically, therein lies its very weakness as a source for Doomsday prediction. In other words, because it is unique, its potential as prophecy is not reinforced by other Maya texts; when it is placed in the context of other such texts, its significance weakens. Monument 6 tells us very little of what was to happen on December 21, 2012. Why? Because that was not its purpose. Thus, when we turn to the larger context of Maya texts for clues to better understanding Monument 6, its supposed millenarian significance fades away.

Figure 2.1. *Left*, portion of Naranjo Altar 1: J5–J11; *right*, portion of new La Corona, panel 2: V5–V8. (*Left*, drawing by the authors after Ian Graham; *right*, drawing by the authors after David Stuart.)

Let us explain. When the Tortuguero passage was first tentatively deciphered in 1996, there were no monuments from other Maya cities that were similar enough to Tortuguero's Monument 6 to be helpful. But since then, two Maya texts of a similar genre have been uncovered and translated. One is dated 593 from Naranjo, the other is dated 677 from La Corona (both in Guatemala). All three texts are on stone markers dedicating the completion of a new building. All three provide the dates of that moment of dedication but also cite future dates that mark the end of calendrical cycles. The Naranjo text cites 10.0.0.0.0 (830 in our calendar); the La Corona one cites a series of dates culminating in 9.13.0.0.0 (692). (See figure 2.1, Naranjo on the left, La Corona on the right.)

These are symbolically pleasing, round, cycle-completing dates, like 13.0.0.0.0—or like our Y2K. The La Corona text, like Tortuguero's monument, also evokes a thirteenth cycle—a cycle which, as we have seen, had a cultural resonance among the Maya similar to our millennia. Neither of the Guatemalan monuments leap as far forward as Tortuguero's 13.0.0.0.0 (2012), and the purpose of the future dates is not clear. But there is nothing in the dedicatory texts to suggest the prediction of disaster. On the contrary, one might more reasonably speculate that the intent was something like, "Built in 1900, this will still stand in 2000." The alternative interpretation of the text presented in the previous chapter—which has the God of the Nine seen and displayed "in a great investiture"—further supports this reading of the monument as dedicatory, not prophetic. As David Stuart later noted, "The 'descent' reading was probably wrong to begin with"; the God of Nine was not, in fact, expected to come down at all.

"A great investiture" does not sound very ominous, and it isn't. Indeed, its spirit is arguably the opposite from apocalyptic, invoking longevity and permanence rather than ephemerality and predetermined destruction. A dozen years after he and Stuart first translated the Tortuguero glyphs and speculated that they might be prophetic, Stephen Houston offered a "mea culpa and a rectification"—the text, he admitted, "had nothing to do with prophecy." Stuart concurred. Later asking, "Does the Tortuguero passage say anything meaningful about what will actually happen in 2012?" Stuart firmly answered, "Absolutely not."

But it was too late. The imaginary cat was already out of the bag. The 2012ologists Geoff Stray and John Major Jenkins protested that scholars had been deliberately downplaying Tortuguero's implications for years; because of the professional Mayanists' fear of the 2012 "monster" and their "cliquish," "closed shop" mentality, "a logical deduction of great relevance was ignored, or withheld." Responding to the evidence that the Tortuguero text was in part a building dedication, Jenkins observed that the Maya viewed "house" and "cosmos" as metaphorically linked. The point, broadly speaking, is valid and interesting, but sometimes a building is just a building.

∼

The supposed Maya prediction of the world's end is based on their Long Count cycle. Without the Long Count, there was no 2012. We introduced the Long Count briefly in the previous chapter, but to analyze the 2012 evidence fully, four aspects of this calendar need to be examined in more detail. First, if the end date of 2012 was determined by the placing of the start date, how was that start date selected? Second, how do we know that the Maya Long Count date of 13.0.0.0.0 was December 21, 2012, in our calendar? Third, how widely used and recognized was the Long Count among the Maya? And fourth, do we know what the Maya thought would happen, in calendrical terms, *after* 2012?

Much of the discussion surrounding the significance the Maya supposedly attached to the year 2012 ignores this obvious question: If 2012 was the end of the great Long Count cycle of 5,126 years, how did the Maya figure out when that cycle began? In other words, how did they pick the Long Count's year zero? If the Long Count developed the way our long calendar did—through a series of idiosyncratic decisions, mistakes, and coincidences—then is the approach to 2012 merely "a precisely arbitrary countdown" (as Stephen Jay Gould called the march to Y2K)? In the previous chapter, we mentioned the theory that the Long Count was by its very nature "predictive"—that its cycle was determined by its end date, not its start. This theory was proposed by a few Mayanists decades ago, and 2012ologists such as José Argüelles (1939–2011) and Jenkins made it a foundation stone to their entire 2012 positions. However, it is not widely accepted among Mayanists today, as there is no evidence to support such a theory; it is an intriguing speculation but not one proven by any other text or image among Maya sources.

Instead, two other possibilities are more likely and more widely accepted. In the calendars used in the world today, the zero date tends to refer to a specific historical event, often with a religious significance (such as the birth year of Christ or the year Muhammad left Mecca) or a political one (such as the Japanese calendars' reference to Japan's mythical founding by the Emperor Jimmu, or the reign of the current emperor). The zero date of the Long Count is, in our calendar, 3114 BC. So, did something happen in the Maya area in 3114 BC—politically, culturally, or astronomically—that is reflected in the Long Count? That is too far back for there to be any textual record of events in the Maya world, nor do later texts refer to anything, in particular, happening in that year.

Furthermore, astronomers tell us that 3114 BC was not an especially significant date in terms of the night sky or planetary alignment, so we cannot look to the ancient skies for a satisfactory explanation.

What about the circumstances surrounding the initial use of the Long Count dates, the first time they were carved into stone? Do we know when that occurred, and does that moment offer any clues? The short answer is no. But the earliest examples of Long Count dates recorded come from the first century BC, and Mayanists plausibly speculate that it was created earlier—perhaps a century or two earlier. Archaeoastronomer Anthony Aveni and other scholars propose that, if the Long Count was conceived in the second or third century BC, the Maya may have counted back from the nearest round date—such as 7.6.0.0.0 (236 BC). In other words, they imagined that the world they lived in had been created a few thousand years earlier and dated that creation in order to give the current year a satisfying trio of zeros in a five-place Long Count date. They then structured that count around the number 13, pinning the end of the cycle a couple of thousand years in the future and placing themselves more or less in the middle. As the Long Count birthed, at least in some cities, the Grand Long Count, the scribes calculating those dates likewise were living roughly in the middle, very far indeed from its start or end dates.

This, in our view, is the most credible explanation. In terms of 2012 predictions, the implications are resounding. Simply put, the element of arbitrariness in the placing of the Long Count is such that it alone—all other evidence aside—undermined the credibility of Maya-based 2012 prophecies.

Second, how do we know that the Long Count date of 13.0.0.0.0 was our December 21, 2012? The answer is that we can be fairly certain, but not 100 percent sure. Many scholars have devoted energy to the question of calendrical correlation, and there are at least twenty-seven fully developed correlations, each giving a slightly different date in our calendar for 13.0.0.0.0. The most widely accepted correlation is called GMT, after the Mayanists who contributed to it (Goodman, Martínez, and Thompson). One could argue that there is a smidgeon of reasonable doubt regarding the GMT correlation. Although today's leading Mayanists tend to endorse it fully—as Michael Coe (1929–2019) commented, "There is now not the slightest chance that these three scholars were not right"—it is not, in Stuart's words, "completely airtight."

Third, how widely used was the Long Count? Although it was the grandest cycle in Maya calendrics, it was neither the first nor the last calendar. That is, the Maya developed and used their shorter calendars (the solar year and the 260-day lunar/gestational calendar) for hundreds of years before the Long Count was invented. And they continued to use those other calendars for centuries after the Long Count gradually faded from usage in the ninth century. Its demise was a symptom of the decline of divine kingship. The Long Count and the institution of the sacred ruler, the *k'uhul ajaw*, rose, flourished, and fell together. Both had appropriated religion and cosmic time for political purposes. The great stone-carved dates had glorified the great kings; without the sacred rulers, the counting and the recording of those days had no reason to exist. The last recorded Long Count inscription dates from AD 910—some six centuries before Spaniards arrived in Mesoamerica. The Long Count, therefore, was not extinguished by Europeans but was slowly abandoned by the Maya themselves, when it became politically irrelevant.

Fourth, what did the Maya believe would happen to the Long Count *after* 2012, or 13.0.0.0.0? If that date marked the world's end, did the count, likewise, simply end? There are various possible answers to that question, based on the varying ways in which Long Count dates were recorded on Classic monuments. But none of those variants suggest that 2012 was merely a terminal date. If the Maya of Quiriguá were still recording dates today, for example, they would see the end of the cycle as simultaneously the start of the next one. The Long Count actually records days, so December 21, 2012, is both 13.0.0.0.0 and simply zero (or 0.0.0.0.0). December 22 will be 1 (or 0.0.0.0.1). After twenty days, the date will be 0.0.0.1.0, and so on.

For the creators of Stela 1 at Cobá—the monument with the twenty-four place date recording billions of years—the end of the cycle on December 21, 2012, would have marked a transition from a five-place count to a six-place one. Thus, they would have rewritten 13.0.0.0.0 as 1.0.0.0.0.0, with the next day (December 22) as 1.0.0.0.0.1. Time would not have ended but expanded as it marched on indefinitely—or at least into octillions of years.

The Maya elite who carved dates in the beautiful Classic city of Palenque (in today's Chiapas, Mexico) likewise viewed time—and their world—as existing before and after the Long Count cycle in which they lived. One glyphic text, from the Temple of the Inscriptions, makes the reign of the great king K'inich Janaab' Pakal (known more popularly as Pakal) seem all the more momentous by noting that the eightieth calendar round (or calendrical cycle) anniversary of his accession to the throne would take place eight days after the end of the eight thousand-year Long Count cycle called the *pictun*. This bit of Maya numerological fun records two days in October AD 4772.

Or take the glyphic text, for example, that appears on the building that Mayanists call the Temple of the Cross (figure 2.2). It records the birth of a woman and a man seven to eight years *before* the creation of the long cycle (in 3122 and 3121 BC). The creation itself is momentous but not accompanied by cataclysm or destruction. This is our idiomatic translation of approximately the first third of one of the texts from this Palenque temple. It records the birth of the woman shortly before the dawn of the new cycle and the arrival of a new deity shortly afterward:

> On 12.19.13.4.0 [December 7, 3121 BC], First Lady Sek was born. Five months and eight years after she was born, the era was wrapped up; the thirteen cycles of four hundred years were completed on 13.0.0.0.0 [August 13, 3114 BC]. A year, nine months, and two days after the face of the new era was revealed, Hun Ye Nal Chac appeared in the sky; on 13.0.1.9.2 [February 5, 3112 BC] he dedicated

Figure 2.2. The Temple of the Cross, Palenque. (Photograph by the authors.)

the Raised-Sky House, the Eight Chac House was its holy name, the Home of the North.

This passage has been variously translated and analyzed, and the specific mythology it introduces—the ancestral and divine origins of the Palenque king that had the temple built—is not our primary concern. What matters to us here is the fact that the birth of two mythical ancestral beings bridges the transition from the previous Long Count era to the new one. The date 13.0.0.0.0.0, the day that starts the long cycle to end in 2012, is not a day of apocalypse. It is simply a resetting of the calendrical clock, a milestone to mark time in the distant past. In that past, birth and creation, not death and destruction, were the important events.

Dennis Tedlock, a leading scholar of Maya literature, argues that a goddess is the most common Maya metaphor for the dawn of a new era. In the previous chapter we discussed the final page of the Dresden Codex and its depiction of the Flood; in doing so, we deliberately downplayed the fact that the codex is overwhelmingly not about endings but about cycles (or, put another way, every ending is also a new beginning).

The codex consists of astronomical tables and almanacs, charting the movements of the moon and of Venus, and placing agricultural seasons within the context of planetary movements. Deities act as metaphors for everything, from the planets to the dates of the 260-day calendar. The deity that perhaps best signifies the dawning of a new era is called Ix Ahau Na (or Ix Ajaw Nah), Lady House. Her "house" is in the sky, around Virgo. She is depicted in the codex sitting on her throne in the vault of the sky, receiving offerings (see figure 2.3).

Lady House in the Dresden text, like First Lady Sek in the Palenque text, is not a metaphor of doom; on the contrary, these women represent dawn, creation not destruction. In an alphabetic Maya text from colonial Yucatan (called the *Ritual of the Bacabs*) the equivalent goddess is called Ix Kin Sutnal. Literally meaning "she of the sun's turn" or "the day's turn," we might call her Lady Returning Sun. In the Paris Codex, her animal avatar is a frog taking the sun in his mouth; in the Madrid Codex, she is a frog jumping or diving in the rain. Her time of the year is March, when the rains begin, the frogs appear and start to sing, and corn is planted. As Tedlock puts it, the day 1.0.0.0.0.1 "should be a good time for planting, and for making new starts of all kinds."

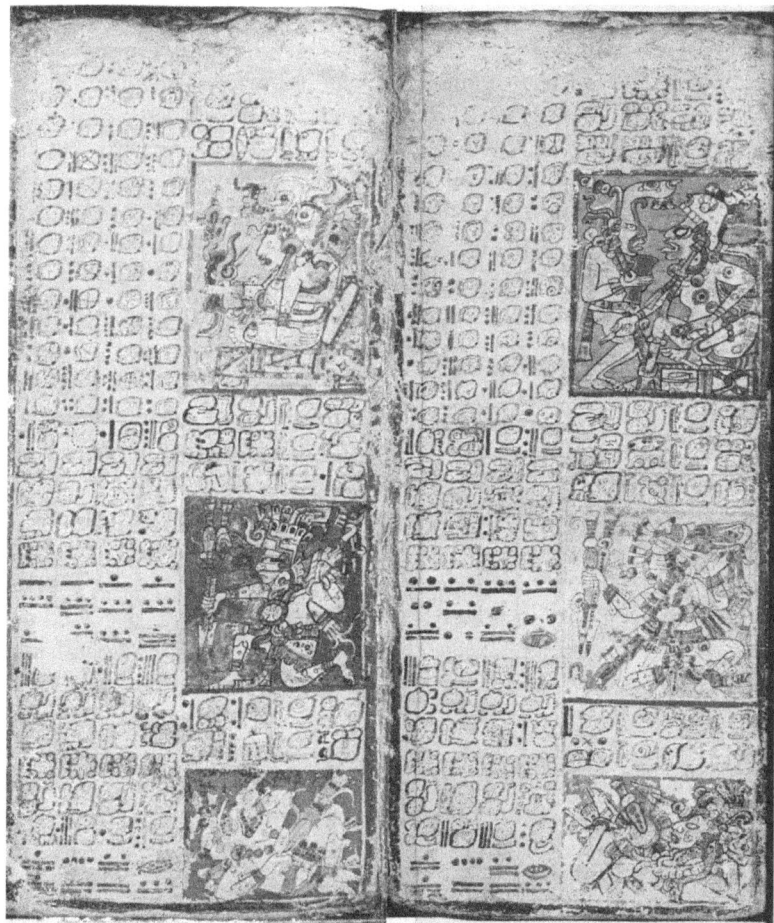

Figure 2.3. Ix Ahau Na (Lady House) from the Dresden Codex, p. 49. (Held by the Sächsische Landesbibliothek, Dresden; image in the public domain.)

∼

The Long Count thus makes for a very shaky foundation for Maya 2012 predictions. But there still remains the issue of Maya millenarianism. By quibbling over the calendar, are we missing the larger point? Did the Maya know that the world in which we live has a limited life span, and are we being imprudent to ignore that knowledge?

The ancient Maya left us an extraordinarily rich array of buildings, stone carvings, paintings, pottery, texts and books using a stunning writing system of about eight hundred glyphs, and other evidence of their cultural accomplishments. Most of this material—certainly the most studied and celebrated structures, monuments, and artifacts—comes from the millennium between AD 200 and 1200. But the complete record of Maya civilization stretches from the fifth century BC up to the present day. If we look at two millennia of that evidence—from the fifth century BC up to the eve of the sixteenth-century European invasion—what impression are we given? Specifically, what seems to have been the primary concerns of the Maya who wrote, painted, carved, designed, and built?

Ask ten Mayanists that question and you will get ten different answers. That caveat aside, we suggest the following six concerns. The first was the fertility of the earth and its agricultural cycles; this is hardly surprising, as Maya society was agrarian, and their diet was based on corn and other crops (occasionally supplemented by wild game and riverine/marine resources). The second was the dovetailing of the natural and supernatural worlds; in a sense, they were one world, occupied by kings, ancestors, religious specialists, people, animals, and the pantheon of gods (introduced in chapter 1)—all dependent upon each other for their survival.

The third was the permanence of place, viewed in highly local terms. There was never an empire that united the Maya, never a language or common sense of identity (again, as introduced in chapter 1). Politics was regional, relations between city-states frequently violent, and cities developed highly local identities. One of the remarkable features of Maya architecture is how distinct and different every major site is from the others. The city was not a city in our sense of the word; its residents lived lives that were similar to those of villagers, working mostly in agricultural production and residing in discrete neighborhoods. But the pyramids, palaces, and temples of the city were seen as deeply rooted in that location, as permanently a part of the fabric of the world as the city's trees and whatever mountains or rivers lay near it.

The fourth was time—the pace of its passing, its observation in the natural world and in the night sky, its measurement and its recording. The continual charting of time was central to agricultural knowledge and to the need to control, as much as possible, the cycles of fertility and growth. Moreover, the domination of time—primordial, mythological, and historical—was central to claims of legitimacy by kings and priests, who had to continually link their own genealogies back to creation events as a means to justify their placement at the apex of the social hierarchy. Time was, no doubt, a source of anxiety (isn't it always?), but it was also the most constant aspect of life on earth; it might seem to pass slowly at times, fly by at others, but the Maya understood that, in reality, its passage was unfailingly uniform.

The fifth concern was aesthetics, how things looked and should look. One could argue that the entire vast corpus of Maya art and architecture was a millennia-long exploration of beauty, an endless investigation into visual sensitivity. Each city-state developed a regional visual style and promoted localized variants of artistic genres: sculpture, painting, and calligraphy. None of the Mayan languages seem to have had, or have, a word for "art"; but, as prominent Mayanist art historian Mary Ellen Miller has put it, "The ancient Maya world was a world of Maya art."

The sixth and final concern of the Maya, we suggest, was humor and play. Every Maya city had at least one ball court, and the ball game is widely illustrated in Maya art. Beyond the ball game, comedy and play of various kinds featured strongly in Maya life. Comic themes in Maya art, many of which we can barely begin to grasp, hint at a whole world of mockery, celebration, and laughter. Maya art is full of humor. Its sculpture and mythology are packed with jokes—ranging from the goofy to the dark, the tongue-in-cheek to the sexual, some with nuances and punch lines that Mayanists have yet to decipher. Maya artist-scribes did not merely compose glyphic texts for purposes of communication, they also reveled in a system that was (in Houston's words) "brimming with evidence of playful invention."

Nowhere in this set of concerns is there a preoccupation with the end of the world, the end of time, apocalypse, extinction, or even an exceptional or unusual focus on death. The most egregious misrepresentation (among many) in Mel Gibson's 2006 movie *Apocalypto* was the styling of the Maya as obsessively and sadistically morbid. Maya life was not overshadowed by death or a fear of the end of time. They did not develop notions of redemption or salvation based on the arrival or return of a leader or deity. To be sure, their complex grasp of calendrics featured a well-developed sense of cyclicity—the cycles of life and death, of planetary movements, and of the agricultural seasons. Furthermore, this included an interest in how catastrophic events, from natural disasters to political violence, might repeat themselves according to similar cyclic rhythms. But almost all the evidence for Maya interest in the cycles of disaster dates from after the Spaniards invaded and introduced Christianity. In general, the Maya were simply not focused on ideas that we would call millenarian or apocalyptic.

Figure 2.4. *The Mayan Empire*: A 2010 educational graphic from boston.com. (Redrawn by Robin Restall after Javier Zarracina; archive.boston.com/bostonglobe/ideas/graphics/20100530_ocean/.)

Popular perceptions of the Maya tend to incorporate outdated misunderstandings of the Maya past—with the Maya often conflated with the Aztecs and both reduced to a kind of millenarian essence. One example is illustrated in figure 2.4, which is drawn from a graphic that appeared in Boston.com in the lead-up to 2012. In the original graphic, the "Mayan Empire" label was accompanied by a caption headed up with "Collapse of the Maya. Before the Year 1000." The caption explained that "the Classic Maya built a powerful society with sophisticated cities and a rich cultural life. War, overpopulation, deforestation, and soil erosion helped hasten its end." The illustrative images are of a pyramid from the Classic Maya city of Tikal and a polychrome rendering of the central portion of an Aztec sculpture called the Calendar Stone (or Sun Stone).

The impression given is one of political centralization, ominous calendrical wisdom, imperial hubris, and millennial collapse. The creator of the graphic and caption should not be blamed for this; it reflects the Mayanist scholarship from decades ago and the persistent, popular impression of the Maya through 2012 and up to today. But the impression is profoundly misleading. The Calendar Stone has nothing whatsoever to do with the Maya (see our discussion of it in chapter 4). There was never a "Mayan Empire" or even Maya empires. There was, indeed, a time of population loss and the abandonment of cities, but that process was gradual, lasting centuries and only affecting specific regions of the Maya area. Mayanists debate whether the term "collapse" is appropriate to this process at all; either way, only by a great stretch of the millenarian imagination was there a sudden "collapse of *the* Maya" (our italics). They did not come to an end "before the year 1000," nor did they live in anticipation of coming to an end in 2012.

∽

If the Maya did not have a well-developed sense of apocalypse, how did the notion of Maya millenarianism get attached to the Long Count cycle? The blame can largely be placed in the hands of early Mayanist scholars—somewhat ironically, as it is professional Mayanists who recently worked hardest to expose the myth of 2012 Maya predictions. Comments by early Mayanists created small snowballs that, over the years, have picked up the flakes of amateur astronomers and Maya devotees, spiritualists and New Age writers, and the many heirs to the West's deep traditions of apocalyptic anticipation; the result was the avalanche of Maya-based 2012 literature.

For example, in a 1957 study of the calendar dates of the Dresden Codex, pioneering Mayanist and astronomy professor Maud Makemson (1891–1977) remarked that "the completion of a Great Period of 13 b'aktuns [i.e., reaching the date 13.0.0.0.0] would have been of the utmost significance to the Maya." This and similar comments were cited over the successive decades and can be found now on websites such as Wikipedia. Makemson's breathless comments on "the astonishing scope of the Maya imagination and inventive powers" were very much a part of the tone of early Mayanism and remain central to the way in which the Maya mystique is perpetuated today.

Makemson represents well the foundations to the giddy relationship between Mayanism and 2012; she found Maya calendrics "awe-inspiring" and said enough along those lines to be used as fodder for 2012 prophecy speculation. But she knew full well that the Maya were not apocalypse-oriented. In fact, she argued that the Maya "invented the Long Count, which was essentially a tally of days since a normal or zero date" in order to give each day a unique name; that is, *not* to highlight a vast cycle or "Great Period" but to deemphasize cyclicity and explore linear dating. Because the calendars invented earlier by the Maya were cycles, each day eventually repeated itself; the Long Count permitted a long-range linearity and unique dating (the way that adding 2012 to December 21 makes that day unique).

Another scholar whose views of 2012 illustrate the development of the phenomenon is Michael Coe. A prominent Mayanist from the 1960s until his passing in 2019, Coe's career spanned the decades of the epigraphic breakthrough—the decipherment of Maya hieroglyphs—a story he documented to much acclaim in his book *Breaking the Maya Code*. In the first edition (1966) of his textbook, *The Maya*, his explanation of the calendar used the term "Armageddon." It had been suggested that "when the Great Cycle of the Long Count reaches completion," wrote Coe, "on the final day of the thirteenth" cycle, "our present universe will be annihilated."

But the glyphs could not be read back then, nor was there a reliable correlation that fixed the Maya day of possible Armageddon in our calendar. Coe suggested December 24, 2011; in the second edition

(1980) of his textbook, that final day was given as January 11, 2013; the fourth edition (1983) of a rival textbook offered December 21, 2012; in his next edition (1984), Coe suggested December 23, 2012. But these contradictions did not mark any sort of controversy; the differences of opinion were part of the unfolding understanding of Maya writing and mathematics, with no one arguing that ancient astronomers actually thought the world would end with the "Great Cycle." In other words, the goal was to try to correlate the calendars—an esoteric intellectual exercise—not to reveal the day of the Apocalypse.

A shift occurred in the 1990s; by Coe's sixth edition (1999) of *The Maya*, he had deleted all speculation about the end of the Long Count's cycle. In the fifteen years leading up to 2012, Mayanists either withdrew from the discussion or issued statements clarifying that the Maya had undoubtedly *not* predicted the world's end. What had changed?

Several factors converged to explain the emergence of 2012 as a Maya-based phenomenon. First, the steady decipherment of Maya writing since the 1970s led to a flurry of exhibitions and publications and helped spur archaeological work in more and more ancient Maya cities, bringing the Maya increasingly into the public consciousness. Second, the analysis of a few specific monuments for the first time—such as the 1996 reading of Tortuguero's Monument 6—drew attention to the notion of Maya calendrics as an apocalyptic puzzle to be solved. Third, the supposed final day of December 21, 2012—now fixed by the GMT correlation and Mayanist consensus as the end of the Long Count's Great Cycle—started to loom in the near future. Fourth, another thread of intellectual speculation—primarily identifiable as New Age and spiritualist thinking—latched onto the Maya as a source of ancient wisdom. We return later (in chapter 6) to the New Age and spiritualist branch of 2012ology, the 2012 Gnostics (as Aveni calls them). For now, our interest is in how such writers combined Maya sources with astronomy to advance 2012ology ideas.

For example, in 1987 José Argüelles helped organize an international "Harmonic Convergence" event, based on the notion that an exceptional alignment of the planets would produce a millenarian moment in August of that year. Argüelles insisted that, based on a convoluted reading of the Aztec calendar, 1987 was the start of the transformation. Its culmination, or galactic "beam end," would be on December 21, 2012; the Maya calendar, he claimed, was aligned to predict and anticipate the galactic convergence. Argüelles took the ancient Maya to be extraterrestrial aliens, and it was their world-transforming return—not Christ's—that he anticipated. During the 1990s, John Major Jenkins picked up this thread and explored it in great detail; his 1998 *Maya Cosmogenesis 2012* was the first book in this exploding genre of literature with the year 2012 in the title. The core notion developed by Jenkins—which he pointed out had been widely misread and abused and then scattered across the Internet—was that the galaxy, or even the universe, would be realigned or altered in a way that would either usher in a new and improved era (Jenkins's position) or destroy Earth. The Maya, with their famous stargazing skills, were credited with anticipating this event.

Most versions of this theory by Jenkins and others center on precession. "Precession" is the astronomical term that refers to how the sun becomes gradually aligned with the Milky Way. The Earth's axis of rotation shifts a little each year, resulting in a slight difference between the solar year (how long it takes Earth to revolve around the sun) and the stellar year (how long it takes the planet to line up with the stars). This phenomenon can be observed without modern technology; it was spotted as early as 128 BC by the Greek astronomer Hipparchus.

It is possible—perhaps likely—therefore, that the Maya were aware of the precession. Jenkins insisted that "there is in fact a great deal of evidence that the ancient Maya were aware of precession," although Mayanists argue that there is nothing in ancient or colonial texts to suggest that they actually recorded or tracked it. Anthony Aveni, in a brilliant summary of the evidence, concluded that the Maya "certainly could have detected precession" but that "there is no evidence to date to support the case that they calculated the cycle, much less even perceived precession as a cyclic phenomenon." Even if we accept the claim that the Maya did try to track it, the precession cycle is about twenty-six thousand years and cannot be predicted through observation to a specific date; at best, one can predict that the alignment will occur within a period of a few centuries, perhaps one century, but not one year—let alone one day.

What of the cosmic map in Stela 25 at Izapa, the significance of which Jenkins tied to his argument that the Maya were well aware of precession? Jenkins asserted that the Izapans—and thus the Maya, although Izapa was not a Maya city—knew that the precession's significance was not just astronomical but spiritual. The next precession, insisted Jenkins, would create an inner alignment in us all, allowing us to "reconnect with our cosmic heart and eternal source"; Izapa reveals that its ancient creators knew this.

Jenkins's take on Izapa made for good reading, and it should not have been dismissed out of hand, but, ultimately, it was not persuasive. To conclude that the Maya associated the precession with the next world creation was to make an enormous interpretive leap. The image on Stela 25 may be a cosmic map and it may indicate a galactic alignment, but the argument is speculative, not substantiated with either internal or contextual evidence.

Furthermore, the Maya were not mapmakers; cartography was one of the few expressions of artistic and spatial representation that the Maya did *not* develop. Amid the vast corpus of ancient Maya art and writing, there is not a single case of a map—not in our sense of the term, in the sense meant by the reading of Stela 25 as a map. When the Maya did start making maps, it was in the early colonial period; the result was a handful of Spanish-influenced, micropatriotic maps, centering on the town of origin and reflecting the highly localized identity of the sixteenth-century Maya (figure 2.5 is a 1557 example, the "round map" from Mani, in northern Yucatan). These are a far cry from star maps; in Aveni's words, they are "*loco*-centric, not *helio*- (sun) or *galacto*-centric."

Finally, even if, for the sake of argument, we were to accept Stela 25 as a unique example of a star map, there is nothing in this image—or any of the other two hundred images from Izapa—that predicts or even suggests a future event. Nor is there any mention of a distant future date, or even any Long Count dates, let alone 2012. We, too, would like to think that over two thousand years ago the builders of Izapa anticipated the future to a degree that had us in mind and that they left us a star map encoded in a drawing of a mythological tale; we're just not convinced that they did.

Another theory, this one with completely imaginary links to the Maya, blames the sun. As in the movie *2012*, the eruption of massive solar flares is imagined as sending solar particles to Earth. In the movie, the poles shifted, there was rapid continental drift, and the planet was swept with tidal waves thousands of feet high. The film did not take itself too seriously, but in his book, *Apocalypse 2012*, Lawrence Joseph predicted earnestly that solar flares would reverse the Earth's magnetic field. The Indian Ocean tsunamis of 2004, and Hurricane Katrina the

Figure 2.5. Gaspar Antonio Chi, *The Mani Land Treaty Map*, 1557 (extant copy from 1600). (Held by the Latin American Library, Tulane University; image in the public domain.)

following year—so the theory went—all anticipated the natural disasters that we should have expected in 2012. The supposed link between Maya wisdom and the threat of the sun was bandied about wildly, especially on Internet sites. But one would search in vain for even the slimmest possible evidence that the Maya predicted a solar event in 2012 or in any subsequent year; there is not even a misinterpretation to be exploded.

∽

We have focused in this chapter on the supposed evidence for end-of-world predictions by the precontact Maya—that is, in sources dating from before the arrival of Europeans in Maya lands in the early sixteenth century. But, as outlined in the previous chapter, there were Maya texts written alphabetically in the centuries after the European invasion, texts that have been interpreted as clearly articulating Maya concepts of apocalypse.

Our contention is that such sources cannot be viewed in the same category as precontact sources; they cannot be seen as simply "Maya," untainted by European cultures and ideas. Books and websites that refer to ancient Maya knowledge—including but not limited to 2012ology writings—are often riddled with a careless treatment of historical periods and geographical regions. But muddling up units of time and space destroys the potential for ancient and historical sources to enlighten us about the past; it prevents the Maya from communicating to us what they really thought.

To highlight the importance of the discrete nature of historical periods and cultural developments in particular regions, we now step away from the Maya—in fact, away from the Americas completely. To understand if and how Europeans altered Maya views of their past and our future, we need to know what kinds of ideas Spaniards brought across the Atlantic Ocean in the sixteenth century. The next chapter, therefore, focuses on medieval Europe. We then return to Mesoamerica, accompanying the Spanish friars, first, to central Mexico (chapter 4) and then back into Maya country (chapter 5).

· 3 ·

God Is Angry

The Millenarian Mother Lode

> I tell you that the Church of God must be renewed, and soon, for God is angry.
>
> —Girolamo Savonarola, apocalyptic Florentine preacher, 1490s

> And we know that we are bound above all to observe all these things by the commandments of the Lord and the constitutions of holy Mother Church. And let him who does not act thus know that he shall have to render an account therefore before our Lord Jesus Christ on the day of judgment.
>
> —attributed to St. Francis of Assisi, thirteenth century

Fame and fortune came to the German artist at the tender age of twenty-seven. Albrecht Dürer had engraved a set of fifteen images, accompanied by text from the Bible. Innovatively, the text acted more as captions to the images rather than the engravings illustrating the text. Published simultaneously in Latin and German, the engravings were an instant success. And a lasting one—they have permanently changed the way in which we see and understand the biblical passages from which they draw.

What were these images? They were first published in 1498, at a time when word of the discovery of a New World across the ocean was circulating in Europe. Did they depict the Garden of Eden, which Columbus thought he had discovered on the coasts of South America? Or did they illustrate conversion and salvation (the New World was populated by peoples who knew nothing of Christianity)? In fact, Dürer selected the Book of Revelation, and his series of engravings was titled *Apocalypse with Pictures*. Europeans loved the German artist's chosen topic—the cataclysmic end of the world—and the pear woodblocks remained a lucrative source of income for Dürer for the rest of his life.

The most famous of the woodcuts is *The Four Horsemen of the Apocalypse*—it soon became Western civilization's most universal and enduring end-of-world image. But the series also included a number of scenes featuring St. John of Patmos, various angels, *The Whore of Babylon*, and three different renderings of reptilian monsters: *St. Michael Fighting the Dragon*; *The Sea Monster and the Beast with the Lamb's Horn*; and *The Apocalyptic Woman* (figure 3.1). The monster images remind one of the great caimans of Maya mythology, vomiting out the Flood in the Dresden Codex, or needing to be slain for the world to be created anew in the *Books of Chilam Balam*. We are not suggesting a causal connection or odd coincidence—the fear of reptiles, especially ones made large and monstrous, is common to human cultures throughout history—but merely noting the interesting parallel. On the other hand, the *Books of Chilam Balam* were written after Dürer's drawings were published (the possible implications of which we shall address in chapter 5).

So how do we explain the success of Dürer's woodcuts? The primal fear of reptilian monsters is not enough, neither would it suffice to investigate the artist's personal religious interests. The explanation lies in the larger culture that provided such fertile ground for the reception of the engravings.

Medieval Europe was in fact a hotbed of apocalyptic imaginings. Fears of the world's end, paired with hopes that a savior would come to replace the flawed world with a better one, developed not only in Mesoamerica and the Mediterranean but also in many times and places in history. But nowhere can match the latter for the depth and frequency of such hopes and fears. In short, Western civilization is the millenarian mother lode.

But, like all cultural developments, European millennialism of the medieval period did not develop in an intellectual vacuum. The theology illustrated by Dürer and debated by innumerable Christian theologians has its root in the older monotheistic religion from which Christianity emerged: Judaism.

∽

Figure 3.1. Albrecht Dürer, *The Apocalyptic Woman*, 1511. (Reproduction courtesy of the Metropolitan Museum of Art. The George Khuner Collection; gift of Mrs. George Khuner, 1968, 68.793.5; image in the public domain.)

Daniel must have been nervous as he was brought before Nebuchadnezzar, King of Babylon (see figure 3.2). Years earlier, in 606 BC, Babylonian invaders had taken Daniel from his home in Jerusalem. Perceiving him to be a smart young boy, his captors had him trained as a court advisor. In time, Daniel developed a reputation as a gifted interpreter of dreams and visions. As the king had been plagued for months by a series of disturbing nightmares, he therefore had Daniel summoned. Despite their best efforts, no one in Nebuchadnezzar's court could determine what the royal nightmares meant. The king had promised that the wise men "will receive from me gifts and rewards and great honor" if they could explain the dreams. But if they continued to fail him, "I will have you cut into pieces and your houses turned into piles of rubble."

Eventually, driven mad with frustration, Nebuchadnezzar ordered the execution of all the kingdom's wise men. At that point, Daniel stepped forward to try his hand. Praying to God, he had a vision in which God explained the dream's ultimate meaning. The resulting description and interpretation of Nebuchadnezzar's dream, preserved in the Old Testament, is one of history's earliest written records of millennial belief.

Daniel vividly described how the king dreamt of a large statue, composed of various types of materials—the head "made of pure gold, its chest and arms of silver, its belly and thighs of bronze, its legs of iron, its feet partly of iron and partly of baked clay." In the dream, Nebuchadnezzar saw a rock, cut out "not by human hands," fall upon the statue, violently dismantling it. Once the statue had been obliterated, a strong wind swept away the debris and the rock grew into a "huge mountain that filled the whole earth." Daniel explained that the different parts of the statue represented a succession of different earthly kingdoms of varying quality. Babylonia was represented by the statue's golden head; Nebuchadnezzar was, after all, the "king of kings." Following the inevitable destruction of Babylonia, interpreted Daniel, another will rise up, of a slightly lesser quality—as symbolized by the statue's silver chest and arms. But the divine rock will also bring this rule to an end. Accordingly, two other even less qualified rulers will come to power, the bronze belly and thighs, followed by the divided kingdom composed of iron and clay, the statue's legs and feet. In the course of this human history, God will be setting "up a kingdom that will never be destroyed," the divinely quarried rock that served to destroy all the earthly kingdoms.

Figure 3.2. Franz von Hauslab the Younger, *Daniel Interprets Nebuchadnezzar's Dream*, 1815–1853. (Reproduction courtesy of the Metropolitan Museum of Art; Harris Brisbane Dick Fund, 1953, 53.600.3520; image in the public domain.)

Daniel not only interpreted the Babylonian king's nightmare but also himself had many dreams that foretold the destruction of earthly kingdoms and the subsequent creation of a divinely led earth. Daniel was not the first person to dream up such ideas; apocalyptic concepts of earthly destruction and re-creation are found in other religious literatures in the Mediterranean and Near East in the centuries before the Christian era. But the story of Daniel and Nebuchadnezzar perfectly introduces the theme of millenarianism in Judeo-Christian civilization for three reasons: first, for its antiquity and lasting popularity; second, because it shows how the notion of cycles of creation was by no means unique to the civilizations developing in Mesoamerica at this time; and third, because it illustrates the relevance of Jewish eschatology—a branch of theology that studies the end of the world—to the Christian millenarian tradition that developed in Europe during the Middle Ages.

According to the Tanakh, the Hebrew Bible, human history will last a mere six thousand years. These six millennia are divided into three periods of two thousand years each. The first period was one of *tohu* (void, or chaos); the second two thousand year period began with the life of Abraham; the third era is that of the messiah, who will come at the start (or during) that final period. Jewish eschatology concerns the appearance of this messiah, who will usher in a new era of human history.

Unlike Christianity, which deems Jesus Christ as a living incarnate of God and thus a divine being, those of the Jewish faith believe that their messiah will not be divine. Instead, the Jewish messiah will be completely human, born of two parents (and thus not of an immaculate conception) and be a descendent of King David. Nonetheless, this human messiah will be capable of uniting humankind; this two-thousand-year Messianic Era will thus be a time of global peace. The birth and revelation of the Jewish messiah terminates the older phase of human history; it will mark the end of the world as we have known it. The signs that the Messianic Era is at hand include the gathering of the Jewish faithful at the Holy Land, a defeat of Israel's enemies, the construction of the third temple in Jerusalem, and the resurrection of the dead. Some sources assert that Gog, king of Magog, will attack Israel, but God will intervene and save the Jewish people. This is the world's final defeat of good over evil. Over the centuries, Gog and Magog have been variously identified—as the Mongol hoards, for example, as Russia, or as Saddam Hussein (during preparations for the 2003 invasion of Iraq,

US president Bush allegedly told French president Chirac that "Gog and Magog are at work in the Middle East").

There have been many false alarms and many claimants to the messianic mantle, but no candidate more successful—thus far, and in some senses—than Jesus Christ. Evolving out of Judaism, early Christianity appropriated and repackaged many older traditions and ideas. Among others, Daniel was brought along for the ride; Jesus himself is quoted as referencing the "end of age" prediction of "Daniel the prophet" when he warns his apostles that after his death God will again return to earth. In fact, during the first few centuries of Christianity, it was commonly believed that Christ himself would return to earth for a thousand years. Hippolytus of Rome (c.176–235) argued that it would be six thousand years before the Second Coming. The idea—called "premillennialism"—that Christ would return in the flesh and remain on earth for those years was declared heresy in the fourth century.

But it persisted, and related ideas flourished as well. In second-century Turkey, the imminent return of Christ was preached by Montanus; although his predictions proved disappointing and the cult was eventually declared heretical by the Church, Montanism spread to various regions of the Roman Empire and lasted for centuries. Even in its barest bones, the Montanist story contains two key elements that have remained central to millenarianism—up to and including the 2012 phenomenon. These are, first, the repeated declaration that the end is nigh, often with a specific given date that inevitably proves to be an anticlimax; failure is explained in terms of miscalculations, the difficulty we have as sinners to understand God's will, or various other excuses leading to the declaration of a new date. Second, the notion that the Apocalypse is imminent inevitably finds fertile ground among the dispossessed, those with the least to lose in the conflagration of Doomsday; the established powers of church and state are more likely to feel threatened. Since Montanus, urgent apocalyptic preaching has tended toward the revolutionary and has been muzzled as a result. Indeed, suppression is part of what gives such ideas their credibility; hence the insistence by some 2012ologists writing outside of academia that university professors were trying to shut them up with denial and derision.

Parallel to the spread of cults such as the Montanists, for the half-millennium leading up to the sixth century, a network of sects across Europe known to us as the Gnostics pursued and promoted the notion that "true knowledge" was the path to salvation. Gnosticism holds that Christians should not simply surrender to faith and accept that most things can only be known by God; instead, they should examine all sources of knowledge, including those of other religions and cultures, in order to uncover the truth. There is a hidden wisdom in the text—or, more likely, in the numbers—waiting to be discovered by the capable and dedicated.

Faced with opposition and eventually violent repression from the Church, Gnosticism increasingly became a movement of covert sages, sacred codes, and tales of ancient wisdom suppressed by corrupt earthly powers. If this sounds like a familiar story, it is probably because you have read or seen the *DaVinci Code* books, movies, and related literature; but it may also be because the spirit of Gnosticism has been very much alive in the twenty-first century (a thread we pick up in chapter 6).

The eschatology that helped define Christianity, particularly that of the medieval period, was partly derived from the Book of Daniel, partly based on the mystical interpretations of events described in the Book of the Revelation of John. Although, through the centuries, clerics and scholars have used the same biblical passages to divergent ends, most understand this section of the New Testament as a vivid, predictive description. It is widely believed within Christian theology to describe what is going to happen at the end of the world, a foreseeing of the world after the destruction of its current form.

The Book of Revelation's depiction of the terrifying events that will come to pass served as fodder for not only graphic artists such as Dürer (see figures 3.1, 3.3, and 3.6) but also whetted the imaginations of medieval period mystics. These closing New Testament passages describe how God's message was given to John via an angel. John has a set of visions, specifically seven messages to seven different churches, all clothed in a cosmic battle between good and evil. After a series of catastrophic events, deserving people are saved by a "Lamb" who destroys the evil in the world by throwing Satan in a pit for one thousand years. This new millennium of peace is often called the "Second Coming of Christ," after a reference in John 14:3 to Jesus' life on earth as his "first coming."

After these thousand years, Satan will be released, some suggest for a seven-year period called the "Tribulation." A massive war between the forces of good and evil will ensue—the oft-cited Armageddon, from

Figure 3.3. Albrecht Dürer, *The Last Judgment, from The Small Passion*, 1509–1511. (Reproduction courtesy of the Metropolitan Museum of Art; gift of Junius Spencer Morgan, 1919, 19.73.206; image in the public domain.)

Figure 3.4. *The Hellmouth*, from the Winchester Psalter, twelfth century. (Reproduction courtesy of the British Library; image in the public domain.)

which Dürer culled his print series. While most human beings will be killed in this struggle, eventually Satan will be defeated. The remaining people who are not true Christians will be sent to Hades during the Last Judgment, another favorite subject of early modern artists (see figure 3.3; Dürer again). Christ will then descend to earth again, during his Rapture. This new era is defined by a unification of the people with God and the linking of the spiritual and the earthly, resulting in a heavenly city called the "New Jerusalem."

Over the centuries, numerous theologians interpreted these biblical passages as apocalyptic foretelling, thereby ensuring that apocalyptic thought would have a lasting effect on late medieval and then early modern philosophy. Indeed, interpretations and images of the Last Judgment are commonplace in medieval literature, art, and on public sculpture. One example—which we have chosen for its artistic merit and because it evokes, again, that universal theme of the fear of reptilian monsters— is the tiny painting of the Last Judgment from the psalter of Henry of Bloise (figure 3.4).

Henry may have used this beautiful prayer book, with its eighty miniature illustrations, on a daily basis. In the psalter's depiction of Judgment Day, the jaws of two beasts form Hellmouth, an apocalyptic image that originated in ninth-century England and remained popular in religious art—and even in theater, as a scary prop device—into the sixteenth century (and we shall see it in Mexico in the next chapter). The appearance inside hell of kings and queens, naked save for their crowns, being torn apart by demons along with others, was central to the potentially radical nature of apocalyptic thinking. One can only imagine that Henry hoped that the final day would not come in his lifetime; he was brother to the English king and Bishop of Winchester from 1129 until his death in 1171.

"The Middle Ages were full of movements driven by specific dates and apocalyptic time frames" (to quote medieval religion scholar Rebecca Moore), many driven by efforts to correlate the six-thousand-year age of the world to the Christian calendar (the *anno domini* that Dionysius Exiguus created in 525). Millenarian fervor—including surges in pilgrimages and relic collection—peaked in AD 500, 801, and 1000. The latter date was obviously made significant by the *anno domini* calendar, which also underpinned millennial excitement around the 1032 or 1033 anniversary of Christ's passion. The famines and plagues of subsequent centuries, especially the Black Death (which took one-third of Europe's population in just seven apocalyptic years in the middle of the fourteenth century), prompted waves of millenarian violence and anticipation.

Probably the best known promoter of millennial thinking in writing was Joachim de Fiore, a late twelfth-century theologian born on the island of Sicily. After making a pilgrimage to the Holy Land at a young age, Joachim returned to the Italian Peninsula and wandered as a hermit before eventually becoming a priest and an abbot under the Cistercian order. The focal point of Joachim's academic work was the interpretation of the Book of Revelation, which he understood as describing an ordered account for all of human history; that he was remembered for his writings on the Apocalypse is reflected in this fifteenth-century woodcut portrait of him (figure 3.5).

Joachim de Fiore divided time into three stages, clearly referencing the symbolism of the Christian trinity, what he called the "Eternal Gospel." The first age was named "The Age of the Father" and was linked to the time period and events recalled in the Old Testament. Joachim described this first age as an era when humans obediently lived in accord with the rules of God the Father. The following human age, "The Age of the Son," began with the birth of Christ. Based on Joachim's interpretation of passages in Revelation mentioning events lasting 1,260 days, he predicted that this second human age would end in AD 1260, commencing his third age, "The Age of the Holy Spirit." This final human era would be defined as a time when humans would be in direct contact with God and finally capable of fully understanding his words. This era would be marked by peace, the creation of an idyllic earthly realm where the authority of the Catholic Church would not be needed.

Joachim's work was both accepted and then condemned during his lifetime, as well as in subsequent years—particularly after 1260 passed without the Apocalypse and the much-hoped-for human union with the Christian godhead (inevitably perhaps, anticlimax and disappointment have become integral to the Western millenarian tradition). But the trying times of late medieval Europe—plague, famine, war—were fertile ground for apocalyptic visionaries. One of the most effective, colorful, and—let's face it—unlikeable was Girolamo Savonarola (1452–1498).

A northern Italian scholar and Dominican friar from a privileged background, Savonarola discovered a talent for what might be called performance preaching. In the Florence of the 1490s he became an

Figure 3.5. Frontispiece to *Vaticinia, siue Prophetiae abbatis Ioachimi, et Anselmi episcopi Marsicani*; Venice: Hieronymum Porrum (and) Giovanni Battista Bertoni, 1589. (Image in the public domain.)

increasingly radical and hysterical public figure, ranting against wealth, power, corruption, promiscuity, and homosexuality. Christian thought was corrupted by an evil kowtowing to Classical scholars; reason itself was an instrument of the devil. The works of Plato and Aristotle, and all those who studied them, should be burned, along with all poetry, one of art's "lowest forms." Savonarola channeled Christianity's millenarian tradition into a series of dramatic, revolutionary sermons, pamphlets, books, and engravings depicting the end of the comfy and wicked world that Florentines took for granted. He spoke of having visions in which "swords, knives, lances, and every weapon" rained down on the people of the city—or the whole peninsula: "I saw a sword, which quivered over Italy, turn its point downward and, with the greatest storm and scourge, go among them and flay them all."

The friar urged the people to repent for their sins immediately, as the end was at hand and "later there will be no room for penitence." Savonarola did not bother offering specific dates for when the Last Judgment would occur; there was no time left for that. He was not the first to claim that the end of the world was already upon us, and—more importantly—he was not the last. His insistence that the end of the world could be divined not by calculations and learning but by opening one's eyes to the preapocalyptic lifestyles of the surrounding world was a notion that has resonated through the centuries since his death (burned at the stake in 1498). Surely, the quasi-scientific arguments for taking 2012ology seriously—the details of Maya calendrics, the analysis of planetary movements—would not have flourished around the turn of the twenty-first century without the fertile ground of modern millenarianism. And, as much as Savonarola was in many ways a medieval figure, he also anticipated the anxiety in the modern West over how and why the world is going to hell in a handbasket. As historian Felipe Fernández-Armesto has put it, Savonarola's

> addiction to millenarianism, his confidence in visions, his prophetic stridency, his hatred of art, and his mistrust of secular scholarship align him with aspects of the modern world most moderns reject: religious obscurantism, extreme fanaticism, irrational fundamentalism. In some ways, the conflicts he brought to a head—the confrontation of worldly and godly moralities, the uncomprehending debate between rational and subrational or suprational mind-sets, the struggle for power in the state between the partisans of secularism

and spirituality or of science and scripture—are timeless, universal features of history. Yet they are also, in their current intensity and ferocity, among the latest novelties of contemporary politics. The culture wars of our own time did not begin with Savonarola, but he embodied some of their most fearsome features.

~

In 1503, Dürer was at it again (or rather, still at it, given his impressive lifetime production). This time, rather than create a series of prints illustrating apocalyptic events, the German artist created multiple engravings detailing the lives of the saints; the success of the engravings helped to popularize in the collective imagination the miracles that gained each saint their renown.

In *St. Francis Receiving the Stigmata*, Dürer depicted the pivotal moment in the life of St. Francis, the miracle that essentially earned him his sanctity (figure 3.6). According to legend derived from an eyewitness account, St. Francis had retreated to Mount Verna (located in the Tuscan region of Italy) in 1224 to fast for forty days. This was intended as a form of corporeal penance but also as an attempt to replicate the self-sacrifice of Christ and his apostles. Suddenly, St. Francis had a "vision of a seraph, a six-winged angel," vividly imaged in the upper left side of the composition, visually prominent as the form is set against the white emptiness of background clouds. This is no ordinary angel but instead a kind of winged crucifix, an image of Christ on the cross aloft with six appended wings. The angel forcefully emits five beams of light that reach down from the heavens and are intercepted by the body of St. Francis himself. The beams conveniently hit five meaningful points within the context of Christian lore—the palms of the saint's hands, the tops of his feet, and the lower right side of his torso—the five places wounded on the body of Christ during his crucifixion. In Dürer's rendition, this violence causes Francis to throw his head back, presumably in pain, but also to look upward toward his assailant.

Despite St. Francis's obvious discomfort, the only person to witness the miracle, Brother Leo—shown in the image's middle ground, warily watching the event out of the corner of his eye—recounted that "this angel gave him the gift of the five wounds of Christ." In phrasing the wounds as a "gift," Brother Leo summarizes the entire purpose and intention of the religious order founded by St. Francis: the emulation

Figure 3.6. Albrecht Dürer, *St. Francis Receiving the Stigmata*, 1503. (Reproduction courtesy of the Metropolitan Museum of Art; Rogers Fund, 1931, 31.58.1; image in the public domain.)

of the life of Christ and his apostles. A few centuries later, the Franciscans would spearhead the Christian campaign against Aztec and Maya cultures. Of all the religious orders that ended up in the Americas, the Franciscans maintained the most profound and well-articulated millennial ideology, and their order was the branch of the Church that most heavily influenced the later millennial traditions of the New World (as we shall see in the two chapters to follow). A short foray into the order's origin and core beliefs is thus necessary.

Legends surround both the early life and later religious experiences of St. Francis of Assisi (1182–1226), but we will summarize the main points here. Born in Italy to a wealthy merchant family, Giovanni Francesco di Bernadone showed signs of disillusion with the material world at an early age. Rather than follow in his father Pietro's footsteps and amass wealth via international trade, a series of ecstatic visions prompted Francesco to dedicate his life to the poor. In his twenties he performed various acts of charity, such as tending to lepers and begging for alms in the name of poverty. According to his life accounts, hearing one sermon in particular changed the course of the young Francesco's life. The priest spoke of how Jesus had told the apostles to live as paupers, to "heal the sick, raise the dead, cleanse those who have leprosy, drive out demons," and to preach that "the kingdom of heaven is near."

After this sermon, Francis decided to fully emulate the apostles, dedicating himself to a life of poverty and proselytizing on the imminence of the "the kingdom of heaven." Donning a simple woolen robe, and without shoes, money, or other means, Francis began preaching. Others followed suit, and in 1209 Pope Innocent III granted Francis and his group of eleven like-minded men permission to start a new religious order. They would be known as the "Order of the Friars Minor." They followed a truly ascetic lifestyle, defined by abstinence from most worldly pleasure—including, but certainly not limited to, food, sex, and physical comforts. As stated later in the order's rule of 1223:

> The brothers should appropriate neither house, nor place, nor anything for themselves; and they should go confidently after alms, serving God in poverty and humility, as pilgrims and strangers in this world. Nor should they feel ashamed, for God made Himself poor in this world for us. This is that peak of the highest poverty which has made you, my dearest brothers, heirs and kings of the kingdom of heaven, poor in things but rich in virtues.

The purpose of the rule was to bring the order's members in closer communion with God so as to better prepare themselves—and those to whom they preached—for the Second Coming, as referenced in the introductory quote. The Franciscans were, in other words, mystics, believers in the power of prayer and lifestyle to achieve direct contact with God. Medieval Franciscan mysticism's two apexes were, in the words of a venerable historian of the order, "the image of the Apocalypse and the sanctification of poverty." From the thirteenth to sixteenth centuries, the Franciscans appropriated, developed, and in many ways embodied the millennium-old Western tradition of Messianic and prophetic mysticism.

This tradition did not end in the sixteenth century—in fact, it was stimulated by the rise of Protestantism, invigorated by the rise of capitalism and the scientific revolution, and survives in multiple forms today, not least of which was the 2012 phenomenon. But what is just as significant to the thread of our argument here, perhaps more so, is the fact that the final great flowering of medieval apocalyptical mysticism and missionizing took place in the Americas. Who led the spiritual assault upon pagan faith in the Americas? The Franciscans. When the first Europeans reached major civilizations in the Americas, whom did they contact? The peoples of Mesoamerica—the Aztecs and other speakers of Nahuatl, the Mixtecs and Zapotecs, and the Maya.

∽

There is a vast literature on millenarianism in the Mediterranean in the thousands of years leading up to the European encounter with, and subsequent settlement of, the Western Hemisphere; what we have offered here is a potted history designed to hammer down one simple point. Whereas millenarianism is not easily and clearly found in ancient Maya civilization, it is *deeply* rooted and ubiquitous in Western civilization. Whereas Maya notions of world-ending apocalypse are muted and obscure, the Apocalypse—with a capital "A"—was a profound and pervasive presence in the medieval West. The contrast could not be starker. We were told that the Maya predicted the world's end in 2012. Yet, as we saw in the previous chapter, Maya culture is a Doomsday dead-end; it is the West that is the millenarian mother lode.

Furthermore, apocalyptic anxieties mounted in Europe in the decades leading up to the Spanish invasion of the Americas. The European encounter with the "New World" served only to encourage such concerns, while the arm of the Church that led the spiritual assault upon the Aztecs, Mayas, and their neighbors was one of the orders most deeply imbued in apocalyptic ideology. It is that story—the impact of the Franciscans upon Indigenous cultures, and, ultimately, 2012ology—to which we now turn.

· 4 ·

The Moctezuma Factor

The End of the World Comes to Mexico

> The Most High was pleased to display before us a continent, new lands, and an unknown world.
>
> —Amerigo Vespucci, 1504
>
> The Middle Ages sang its swan song in the New World in the sixteenth century.
>
> —John Phelan, *The Millennial Kingdom of the Franciscans in the New World*, 1956
>
> For a time, I have been concerned, looking toward the mysterious place from whence you have come, among clouds and mist . . . and now it has come true, you have come. Be doubly welcomed, enter the land, go to enjoy your palace; rest your body. May our lords be arrived in the land!
>
> —words that Moctezuma, emperor of the Aztecs, allegedly spoke to Hernando Cortés, 1519

The Aztec Empire was defeated not by Spanish invaders but by the millenarian beliefs of the emperor, Moctezuma. The great Mexican empire was rapidly destroyed not by Cortés the conquistador but by Quetzalcoatl, an Aztec god. This, at least, was the story told by both Spaniards and Aztecs in the sixteenth century, and it has persisted at the heart of narratives of the Conquest of Mexico to this day.

The kernel of this interpretation of the Conquest is the tale of an ancient king who ruled the Mexican kingdom of Tula centuries before the rise of the Aztecs (the name popularly used for the Nahuas of central Mexico who forged the empire that we likewise call Aztec; the empire's dominant city-state was Mexico-Tenochtitlán, whose inhabitants called themselves Mexica). Named Quetzalcoatl (Feathered Serpent), he fell from power and went into exile. But rather than dying, he became divine and was destined to return. A feathered serpent deity had been worshiped in Mesoamerica for centuries, perhaps millennia; the Maya called him Kukulcan or Kucumatz (which likewise means "feathered serpent" in Yucatec and K'iche' Mayan). So, the legend of the exiled ruler merged with the mythology of Quetzalcoatl, god of wind and knowledge (figure 4.1 is one rendering of the god in a sixteenth-century codex).

Hernando Cortés told the Spanish king, in a letter written in 1520 (in the middle of his two-year war of invasion against the Aztecs), that Moctezuma himself told him a version of this tale. The people of Mexico had always believed, said the emperor, that the descendants of this ancient ruler "would come and subjugate this land and take us as their vassals." Moctezuma continued to Cortés (the conquistador claimed):

> So according to the place from which you say you come, which is where the sun rises, and the things you tell us of the great lord or king who sent you here, we believe and we are certain that he must be our natural lord, especially because you say that he has known of us for a long time. So be assured that we will obey you and will hold you as lord in place of that great lord of which you tell us.

Cortés not surprisingly made much of the idea that Moctezuma greeted him either as a *returning* lord or as the representative of the ruler for whom the Aztecs had been waiting. The idea enlisted the supposedly superstitious beliefs of the Aztecs to give credence to the otherwise improbable claim that the emperor had not only welcomed Cortés but also immediately surrendered to him. The letter quoted above was available in print in Spain as early as 1522, so the story of the emperor's speech of surrender rapidly became common currency in narratives of the invasion wars, soon styled as the "Conquest of Mexico."

It has remained so up to the present, with Conquest-era judgments on Moctezuma reverberating loudly in modern histories. For example, the famous juxtaposition written in 1543 by Juan Ginés de Sepúlveda

Figure 4.1. *Quetzalcoatl*, from the Codex Telleriano-Remensis, folio 10r, sixteenth century. (Held by the Bibliothèque Nationale de France, Paris; image in the public domain.)

of "a noble, valiant Cortés with a timorous, cowardly Moctezuma" was echoed in Barbara Tuchman's classic 1984 study of the failure of leadership from the Trojan Horse to the disaster of Vietnam. The Aztec emperor, she wrote, was a "fatal and tragic example" of the folly and "mental standstill" that can paralyze a ruler:

> Through an excess of mysticism or superstition, he had apparently convinced himself that the Spaniards were indeed the party of Quetzalcoatl come to register the break-up of his empire and, believing himself doomed, made no effort to avert his fate.

Put another way, in a line read and no doubt swallowed as fact by the many readers of Jared Diamond's Pulitzer Prize–winning *Guns, Germs, and Steel* (1997): "Montezuma miscalculated even more grossly when he took Cortés for a returning god."

Do we only have the victors' version of the Spanish invasion, the West's view of events running consistently from Cortés to Diamond? In fact, there are also some accounts written down in the sixteenth century in Nahuatl (the language of the central Mexicans, Aztecs included), giving us potential insight into the Aztec perspective. The best known of these, a passage from an epic work later dubbed the Florentine Codex, reproduces Moctezuma's speech of welcome: *Totecuioe oticmihiovilti, oticmociavilti, otlaltitech tommaxitico,* began the emperor, "Oh our lord, be doubly welcomed on your arrival in this land!" Standing tall before the conquistador, face to face, Moctezuma went on:

> You have come to satisfy your curiosity about your city-state of Mexico, you have come to sit on your seat of authority, which I have kept a while for you, where I have been in charge for you, for your agents the rulers who have gone, who for a very short time came to be in charge for you.

Naming the five emperors who ruled the Aztec domain before him, Moctezuma depicts Cortés himself as the legitimate lord of the empire; the preceding century of emperors have merely been regents, keeping the throne warm for its true holder.

The story of Moctezuma's supposed superstition-inspired surrender of the Aztec Empire to a few hundred Spaniards is not the red herring to our tale that it might seem to be. The terms used by Tuchman—for example, "doom," "fate," and "mysticism"—are the language of millenarianism. The conventional narrative has Moctezuma undone by belief in the power of prediction. There is even an astronomical component to the story; Moctezuma's nerves are undone by a series of bad omens, the first of which is a comet, "a flaming ear of corn" seen in the sky (see figure 4.6 at this chapter's end). The implication is that the Aztecs had developed millenarian beliefs and expectations, that these were deeply rooted in central Mexican cultures, and that they were so important as to potentially influence major events—such as the collapse of the greatest empire the region had seen. Either this was true (and we search for 2012 roots in central Mexico) or it was not (and we search for the roots of the Moctezuma millenarian myth).

As the sun set on the volcanoes and lakeside towns of the Basin of Mexico, a procession of Aztec priests left the great plaza at the heart of the Aztec capital. With the towering temple-pyramids of Tenochtitlán's ceremonial center at their backs, they walked across the causeway that linked the island-city to the eastern banks of Lake Texcoco. There they climbed the gentle slope of the small mountain of Huixachtlán (Hill of the Star) to the temple at its summit, where they could be seen from almost anywhere in the Basin.

The Aztec Empire was dark; all fires had been extinguished in preparation for the ritual then unfolding. As midnight approached, the Basin's hundreds of thousands of inhabitants climbed on walls, rooftops, and hills, anywhere that gave them a view of Huixachtlán. As Orion's Belt—the Fire Drill constellation—became visible in the evening sky, priests removed the heart of a sacrificial victim and placed a fire drill in his chest cavity. The victim was chosen through a careful selection process; his name had to contain the term *Xiuitl*, which means both "fire" and "year" in Nahuatl. In this Xiuitl's chest, sparks were made, then a small flame, then the first fire of the new fifty-two-year calendar round. Light returned to the empire. Soon, a great bonfire was created, into which bundles of sticks were thrust, turned into torches, and taken down into the city to light fires in the temples (see figure 4.2). They began with the two great temples to the deities of war and rain, then took the flame to lesser temples, to private homes in the city, and finally out to the temples, towns, and villages of the empire.

Figure 4.2. *The New Fire Ceremony*, from the Codex Borbonicus, p. 34, sixteenth century. (Held by the Bibliothèque de l'Assemblée Nationale, Paris; image in the public domain.)

This ritual—known to us as the New Fire Ceremony—took place in Mexico, in some form or another, every fifty-two years for at least a millennium. The one described above, the only one for which we have written and visual evidence (such as the Codex Borbonicus, excerpted in figure 4.2), was the last New Fire Ceremony ever enacted. It was held in 1507, five years after Moctezuma became emperor. It symbolizes two important perspectives on Aztec history—two points that allow us to dismantle and correct the impression given by the narrative that began this chapter.

The first point is about how the Aztecs viewed the turn of the calendrical cycle. Did the Aztecs fear that without the New Fire Ceremony to initiate the next fifty-two years, their world would end? Most likely not. There is no doubt that such rituals were taken seriously by the Aztecs and other Mesoamericans, that they were seen as vital and efficacious. But there is little sign that Mesoamericans anticipated the end of the next cycle with great anxiety or with the expectation that it would impact them and their families. In other words, rituals like the New Fire Ceremony were celebrations of renewal and rebirth, not manifestations of millenarian concern.

For the Aztecs, this lack of concern can be largely explained by the vagueness of the larger cycle. For one thing, the Aztecs had no equivalent to the Maya Long Count. There is no evidence that a long count was ever recorded in central Mexico and (as we saw) even the Maya one had fallen into disuse half a millennium before the rise of the Aztec Empire. Furthermore, whereas the Maya believed they lived in the fourth creation of the world, the Aztecs believed their present to be the fifth. Not only that, but the previous creations were of varying lengths. The first was 676 years (thirteen cycles of fifty-two years), the second 364 (seven cycles of fifty-two), the third 312 years (six cycles), and the fourth back to 676 years. So how long was the fifth cycle to be? The Aztecs believed that earthquakes would mark the sixth creation of the world, but there was no apparent consensus or common belief as to how long the fifth cycle would be.

Aztec notions of these great cosmic cycles are illustrated on the Calendar Stone, perhaps the most easily recognized art object created in the Indigenous Americas (figure 4.3). This monumental sculpture measures twelve feet across, is four feet thick, and weighs more than twenty-four tons. It likely functioned as a small platform, viewed from above. Iconographically complex, the sculpture was originally brightly painted. Composed of a series of concentric rings, the central ring hosts the outward-looking face of the Aztec sun or earth deity, whose outstretched fists hold human hearts. (Scholars debate which deity is depicted; recent interpretations include art historian and archaeologist Susan Milbrath's identification of the face as that of solar deity Tonatiuh, and David Stuart's assertion that it is both the sun god and a portrait of Moctezuma as a sun king.)

Surrounding this god, four dates are illustrated, each of which commemorate the day on which the previous four eras ended cataclysmically. The first era, represented in the square cartouche in the upper right, is symbolically referred to by the date of 4 Jaguar, recalling when

Figure 4.3. The Calendar Stone, 1479. (Held in the Museo de Antropología e Historia, Mexico City, Mexico; photograph by the authors.)

the era's inhabitants, immense giants, were violently destroyed by fierce wild cats. The world was created anew but then succumbed on the date 4 Wind due to hurricanes, as seen in the upper left square cartouche. The era 4 Rain followed, represented in the lower left square cartouche, when a horrific rain of fire consumed the world. The fourth era, 4 Water, as seen in the lower right cartouche, came to an end after a flood had destroyed life on earth. This brings us to the fifth era, one that will supposedly end on the date 4 Earthquake; the Doomsday event will be—you guessed it—a massive geological tremor.

It is easy to see how this monument has been used, more than any other Aztec text, sculpture, or art, to illustrate the supposed millenarianism of the Aztecs. It does refer to the Aztec idea of previous eras of creation, each of which was destroyed rather violently. But nowhere on the monument (nor anywhere in any form or expression of Aztec culture) is there evidence that the world would not begin anew.

In fact, the very ideology of time as a series of cycles marked inevitably by renewal is represented elsewhere in the monument itself. In addition to the four dates described above, two other dates are carved on the monument. The date 1 Flint Knife, located near the middle of the image, had both cosmological and political importance to the sculpture's Aztec audience: it referenced the time when the Aztecs began their migration from their mythological place of origin, Lake Aztlan, and was also the date (in 1428) when they defeated a rival Basin of Mexico population (the Tepanecs), allowing the Aztecs to ascend to power. The other additional calendrical date, 13 Reed, refers both to the creation date of the current world and to the moment when the first Aztec emperor, Itzcoatl, ascended to the throne by defeating another rival city-state in the Basin, Azcapotzalco.

The purpose of these pairings is transparently political and decidedly not apocalyptic; Aztec imperial ideology was well-developed, sophisticated, and "sold" to the empire's subjects in multiple complex packages, the Calendar Stone being just one example. The references to 1 Flint Knife and 13 Reed linked mythical events from the deep past, or mythistory, to military and political triumphs achieved recently and locally by the Aztecs; the empire's rulers thereby claimed that Aztec hegemony was as much a fact of life—and just as legitimate—as the world itself. The message was: Aztec rule is an integral facet of the current world, as it should be; this world is not about to end; on the contrary, it and its rulers are here to stay, to see out the cycle and—think of the New Fire Ceremony—to not only survive but also manage the transition to the next cycle.

One final point about the misuse of the Calendar Stone: it has been appropriated to illustrate calendar-based millenarianism not only among the Aztecs but also among the Maya. The stone adorned 2012 books, novels, websites, and a multitude of other graphic formats. We have already seen two such examples—the newspaper illustration that is our figure 2.4 and the *Bizarro* cartoon that is our figure I.1; the fact that the Calendar Stone's misuse in the cartoon is irrelevant (the joke still works) reflects how common the misappropriation of the image has become. But, of course, the Calendar Stone has no bearing on anything Maya. Aztec and Maya cultures are both part of Mesoamerican civilization, but they are separate and distinct from each other. The Calendar Stone was carved in the Basin of Mexico (possibly in 1479, but probably during Moctezuma's reign of 1502–1520), many hundreds of miles and hundreds of years from anything even remotely related to the supposed Maya 2012 materials.

The second point to be made here, stemming from the New Fire Ceremony, is about Moctezuma himself. The ceremony of 1507 was an example of how well the Aztecs appropriated old traditions for the religious and political purposes of their empire. By laying claim to the control of the calendar, they helped perpetuate their control over some sixty city-states across half a million square kilometers in central and southern Mexico—the entity we call the Aztec Empire. The 1507 ceremony also promoted the authority and legitimacy of Moctezuma's dynastic lineage. His portrait as the sun king on the Calendar Stone (assuming Stuart is right), does the same work. The later portrayal of him as ineffective, hesitant, and even cowardly in the face of the Spanish invasion does not correlate with his record as ruler.

In fact, he was one of the empire's most dynamic and effective leaders, waging a series of successful campaigns to expand the empire south into what are now Oaxaca, Chiapas, and the Isthmus of Tehuantepec. Had it not been for the Spanish invasion, it would likely have been the captains of Moctezuma, not Cortés, who would have led Aztec warriors into Maya lands in the 1520s and 1530s; a 1559 New Fire Ceremony would likely have symbolized Aztec control over most of what is today Mexico and Guatemala. The Calendar Stone and the New Fire Ceremony not only illustrate Aztec imperial ideology but also specifically reflect Moctezuma's assertion of an awesome authority, one imbued with the powers of creation and cosmic-level control over the cycles of the calendar.

What, therefore, of Moctezuma's surrender to Cortés without a fight, his speech of submission recorded in Spanish and Nahuatl sources alike? We have, as you will have anticipated, a different interpretation of the emperor and his meeting with the conquistador (in short, that surrender is a Spanish invention). But first, we must turn to the Franciscans and their arrival in the Americas.

∽

It is somewhat mind-boggling to think that while the Aztecs were engaged in the New Fire Ceremony in 1507, a short distance to the east the Spaniards were a decade and a half into the exploration and settlement of the Caribbean; yet neither knew of each other's existence or the impact their mutual discovery would make on the world. Since Christopher Columbus had first returned to the Old World, in 1493, Europeans had wrestled with how to accommodate his findings to their worldview. The initial effect was less than dramatic: Columbus himself insisted that he had found islands off the coast of East Asia, and the newness and extent of the discoveries was not widely promoted until the next decade, mostly by Amerigo Vespucci. For example, the Florentine voyager's *Mundus Novus* of 1504 popularized the term "New World" and anticipated how church scholars would interpret the discoveries. Take the description of one of Vespucci's Atlantic crossings, which allegedly took sixty-seven days, of which forty-four were

> of constant rain, thunder and lightning—so dark that we never did see sun by day or fair sky by night. By reason of this, such fear invaded us that we soon abandoned all hope of life. But during these violent tempests of sea and sky, so numerous and so violent, the Most High was pleased to display before us a continent, new lands, and an unknown world. At sight of these things, we were filled with as much joy as anyone can imagine usually fall to the lot of those who have gained refuge from varied calamity and hostile fortune.

The tone of the piece is one of apocalypse and redemption. The ocean's watery grave and the totality of the tempest are a metaphor for the end of the world; the God-given New World is a metaphor for the idyllic millennium that follows. The voyagers are saved, and the new lands are the reason for their salvation.

The message was clear; Columbus had said it too: the New World was delivered to Christians for a purpose. Because the Bible makes no mention of the Americas, the use of the scriptures to make sense of their existence required some imagination. Not surprisingly—at least, according to our argument here—the discoveries across the Atlantic soon fed into Europe's long-standing fascination with the drama of the Apocalypse. This was largely thanks to a popular biblical exegesis circulating at the time. Nicholas de Lyra (1270–1349) was a French Franciscan and a professor at the Sorbonne in Paris; there he wrote what is sometimes called the world's first commentary on the Bible. The commentary was not printed until 1471, but it was an instant and wild success, owned and repeatedly cited by historical figures such as Columbus and the influential Dominican friar Bartolomé de las Casas. For our tale, Lyra's interpretation of the Gospel of Luke is particularly pertinent, as it contains the biblical passage that would be most commonly used to justify the New World evangelical campaign.

In chapter 14 of Luke, Jesus, while a guest at the dinner table of "a prominent Pharisee," recounts a parable of a rather different dinner party. A stately lord was planning a banquet, and he called upon his servant to invite three guests to dine. One by one the guests declined, citing various excuses. The first had to look at a newly purchased field, the second had to try out a new head of oxen, and the third could not attend because he had recently been wed. Returning with these regrets, the servant was again dispatched by his master but this time ordered to "go out quickly into the streets and alleys of the town and bring in the poor, the crippled, the blind, and the lame." The servant returned with these new guests, and when there was still room at the banquet table the lord ordered the servant to have it filled—so as to exclude the original guests, so that "not one of those men who were invited will get a taste of my banquet."

While this parable was told by Jesus as a means to teach a morality lesson on the importance of charity, in the millennial hotbed of medieval Europe it was transformed into a veiled reference to the world's impending doom. Under Lyra's pen, the lord became symbolic of Jesus Christ himself, dinnertime became the end of the world, and the banquet feast was the inevitable eternal bliss. And what of the other players in this parable? The servant came to represent the priests of the world, who call the masses to partake of the feast; and the three guests who refused to partake were obviously references to the three pagan populations of the medieval world: the Jews, the Muslims, and the Gentiles.

The discovery of the Americas and its millions of Indigenous inhabitants presented a massive, previously unknown population of Gentiles. As one of the principal prophesies of the Second Coming was the necessary conversion of all people on earth—and thus the creation of a truly universal Christianity—this seemingly impossible task was now deemed possible. The last unconverted population could now be accounted for. The time had come.

More so than the discovery of the islands in the 1490s, the realization in the 1520s that there was a vast, heavily settled mainland resounded loudly among the religious orders in Spain, especially the Franciscans. Symbolic of their response was the fact that the order sent a dozen friars—an Apostolic Twelve—into central Mexico in 1524. The head of the Franciscans in Spain instructed the Twelve to immediately begin the proselytization of its millions of Nahuas (Nahuatl speakers) and other native peoples, "to convert by word and example" those who "are held captive with the blindness of idolatry under the yoke of Satan."

Ca yehuantin huel achtopa hualmohuicaque, "These were the very first who came," the Nahua scribe of Puebla later wrote, listing their names and adding that "they brought here the holy things of our lord God." In nearby Tlaxcala, the entry in the town annals was the same: "Reed year. Here in this year the twelve friars came. They brought the holy things of our lord God. . . . They were the ones who brought the faith, the Holy Gospel." The "things" were the sacraments; the new lord God had a name, written *Dioz* by Puebla's scribe; the new faith was the *Sancto Euagelio*. Tlaxcala had been an enemy of the Aztecs, resisting the empire for decades and then playing a central role in its destruction. But they did not replace the Aztecs; along with the Aztecs, who were fellow Nahuas (Nahuatl-speakers), the Tlaxcalans became subjects of New Spain, subjects of the new Church. The new faith had come to replace the old one, as a later entry in the Tlaxcalan annals remarked, "5 Reed year. At this time the friars arrived. Then was the time that the devils' houses were demolished." The temples fell, the pyramids were decapitated, and in their place the new churches rose.

The conversion process—the Spiritual Conquest, as it became known—was not, of course, quite that simple. And, despite early claims of God-given successes on a vast scale, the Franciscans knew that the task was a challenge of epic proportions. The effect was to encourage the blossoming of millenarian justifications and expectations, especially as the decades passed and it became clear that this particular conquest was going to last generations. A "mystical interpretation of the conquest" emerged (in the words of one scholar), best exemplified by Gerónimo de Mendieta, a Franciscan whose take on the process was heavily influenced by Nicholas de Lyra's reading of Luke's gospel. Mendieta arrived from Spain in 1554 and dedicated his whole life to converting central Mexico's Indigenous peoples. His monumental account of the conversion campaign, titled *Historia eclesiástica indiana* (The History of the

Church in the Indies), used the parable in Luke to explain the entire Spiritual Conquest.

Thanks to Lyra, the parable was already being read as a veiled reference to the Apocalypse and the Second Coming of Christ. Mendieta likewise saw the host as Jesus Christ and the meal as symbolizing "eternal happiness," with the mealtime as the end of the world. But while he accepted that the guests who refused to come to the banquet table represented the three unconverted populations of the early modern world—the Jews, the Muslims, and the Gentiles—Mendieta took his interpretation a step further. In his view, the three invitations are clues intended to refer to the different methods of conversion that friars should take when proselytizing to people of the three un-Christian faiths.

This highly pragmatic rereading of the banquet parable gave practical advise on how to convert the remaining unconverted—all with the goal of bringing on the Second Coming. As Mendieta explained:

> By means of His illuminations, warnings and punishments, by means of His servants the patriarchs and prophets, by means of His own son in person and later by means of the apostles, the martyrs, the preachers and the saints, God has been calling all the peoples of earth to hasten to prepare themselves to enter and to enjoy that everlasting feast that will be endless. This vocation of God shall not cease until the number of the predestined is reached, which according to the vision of St. John must include all nations, all languages and all peoples.

Mendieta surmised that since both the Jews and Muslims had prior knowledge of the scripture, their conversion should be relatively easily. The Gentiles, on the other hand, had no prior knowledge of the word of God and thus posed the greatest challenge. In the Luke parable, the host sent his servant to take to the streets and "make them come in"; Mendieta read this to mean that the "pagan" Indigenous population of the Americas had to be converted by force if necessary. This meant a strong paternal presence rather than violence: "The Gentiles should be compelled in the sense of being guided by the power and the authority of fathers who have the faculty to discipline their children."

The imposition of that authority took many forms, with mixed results. In the end, the Nahuas and their neighbors played as much of a role in the conversion process as did the friars and other Spanish priests. Nahuas, Mayas, and other Mesoamericans were not passive recipients of Catholicism; they accommodated and appropriated it in ways that made sense to them. The result was the formation not just of a Mexican Catholicism but of many localized Catholicisms. The key point here is that embedded in that process were millenarian ideas such as those articulated by Mendieta. The friars believed that their primary role was to prepare the inhabitants of the new continent for the impending coming of Christ.

Their new parishioners, seeking to make sense of the violence of the invasion wars and the decimation of one pandemic after another, wondered if Spanish friars and colonists were not themselves harbingers of this urgently anticipated Apocalypse. Two Aztecs who survived the invasion wars to become baptized, Nahuas named Martín Ocelotl and Andrés Mixcoatl, rejected the new faith while borrowing its millenarian message; they drew Indigenous followers (and the condemnation of the Inquisition in the 1530s) with their apocalyptic anticlericalism and vision of a Christian-free millennial age. According to Mendieta, a nine-year-old Nahua named Ana proclaimed in 1574 that the endless, deadly cycle of epidemic disease was a sign from God that the Apocalypse was already underway. There are numerous examples of this kind for the sixteenth and subsequent centuries; the Franciscans had provided Indigenous Mexicans with a framework of explanation for man-made and natural disasters, one that was used throughout the colonial period.

To make the point another way, take the example of the mission complex at Actopan, a small Nahua town in central Mexico. It was built by Augustinians, not Franciscans, but the ideological impetus behind it was the same—the friars chose millennialism as the central theme used to adorn the walls of the church's open chapel (figure 4.4), making sure that apocalyptic imagery permeated the visual world of their Indigenous flock. Built in the 1550s, the open chapel was the first completed permanent architecture in the mission town and was where most public masses were held. The structure was not unique to Actopan; in fact, these open chapels were invented to accommodate the large numbers of Indigenous congregants who could not easily fit into the relatively small naves of mission churches. Open chapels were, thus, a standard architectural form used throughout New Spain during the early years of the evangelical campaigns, before warfare and epidemic disease reduced the Indigenous populations to such levels that even the small interiors of the mission churches could accommodate entire villages.

Figure 4.4. The Open Chapel of Actopan, Hidalgo, Mexico, sixteenth century. (Photograph by the authors.)

The open chapel of Actopan is impressive, indeed. It is a relatively simple design, consisting of a monumental barrel vault that terminates in a sheer back wall, forming a massive niche. Halfway up the rear wall of the open chapel, a friar would have stood on a raised podium that hosted a small altar. The lack of paintings on the rear wall most likely approximates the location and size of this platform. From this lofty stage the priest would have delivered stirring, apocalyptic messages to the crowd below.

While the words of the friar's sermons were an ephemeral oration, whose subtelties have been lost in the intervening centuries, the visual culture that surrounds this architectural context provides a permanent record of the sermons' probable themes. The vertical walls of the open chapel are completely covered in multicolored murals that vividly illustrate the themes of the priests' sermons. One can easily imagine an Augustinian friar using the murals as didactic aids, manipulating a long stick to point out specific visual moments to drive his point home to the congregants. The use of "public" art was particularly necessary early on in the Spiritual Conquest, when most of the Indigenous population could not understand Spanish, let alone Latin. The Actopan murals are silent testaments to the Spanish priests' obsession with the impending Apocalypse—and to their efforts to scare their new flock into believing too.

The walls of the open chapel were divided into a gridded pattern with individual scenes inhabiting the created rectilinear spaces. This fortuitously imitated the painting style used to illuminate precontact codices. Viewed as a whole, the mural cycle is a morality tale demonstrating proper behavior for the newly Christianized Nahua parishioners. Some scenes are banal enough—there are images that promote Christian marriage, for example—but much of the mural cycle is devoted to gruesome imaginings. The context of these more violent images is the millennial and apocalyptic flavor of the New World evangelical campaign, as the compositions form an elaborate version of the Last Judgment. While the priest preached of the agonies that awaited the unconverted, the unbelieving, or even the misbehaving neophyte, he was surrounded by horrific scenes of torture, painted to scare the local population into

Figure 4.5. *The Maws of Hell* mural, from the open chapel of Actopan, Hidalgo, Mexico, sixteenth century. (Photograph by the authors.)

submission to the new religion. On the walls are people with brown skin—clearly intended to represent the local Nahuas—being subjected to a variety of tortures; the techniques were the tried-and-true torments of medieval Europe, such as flaying, burning, and stretching on flaming racks.

One scene is particularly harrowing. It is now badly faded, but enough of it can be seen (see figure 4.5): It depicts a massive gaping mouth, an immense blue maw reminiscent of the medieval *Hellmouth* seen in chapter 3, but here reimagined especially for a native audience. It is to this scene that the priest would have pointed as he explained, in full detail, the lasting consequence of un-Christian behavior. On the day of reckoning, one could only expect to be ushered into the depths of hell for all eternity—and for the friars who led the Spiritual Conquest in the New World, that Day of Judgment was coming soon. The message was clear: be afraid; be very afraid.

∼

We left Moctezuma, earlier in the chapter, yellow-bellied and paralyzed by superstition, but with a promise to rehabilitate his reputation. We argued that two sets of contextual evidence undermine the notion that the Aztec emperor was lily-livered: the lack of a strong millenarian or apocalyptic tradition in central Mexican culture; and Moctezuma's aggressive, expansionist track record during the seventeen years of his rule leading up to the Spanish invasion. (There is actually a third line of evidence, which we do not need to follow here: the story of how Spanish conquistadors and chroniclers invented the lie that Moctezuma surrendered and used it to justify the atrocities of their wars of invasion.) Sure enough, a closer look at the sources that painted the image of Moctezuma as a tragic millenarianist date from after that invasion; the portrait is a post-Conquest creation, with roots more in medieval Europe than Aztec Mexico.

For example, in the various versions of the speech that Moctezuma allegedly made to Cortés, the emphasis is on political sovereignty, not the millenarian fulfillment of a religious idea. In the larger passage from which we quoted earlier, Cortés makes no mention of Quetzalcoatl (who does not appear in any of Cortés's letters to the Spanish king), nor does he ever claim that Moctezuma took him for a god. Bernal Díaz del Castillo, a conquistador who claimed to have witnessed the famous meeting, repeats Cortés' account without mention of any gods. Likewise, the Nahua account in the Florentine Codex neither names any deities nor suggests that Cortés is one.

However, in a mid-sixteenth century account by Francisco López de Gómara (not a conquistador but Cortés' secretary in Spain), Indigenous Mexicans initially imagine that all Spaniards are gods. López de Gómara's influential account introduced a number of themes and twists to the tale that are picked up and turned into conventional wisdom for centuries—the apotheosis of the conquistadors is one of them. Furthermore, the notion of Cortés as the returning lord, with its biblical echoes in the tales of the Prodigal Son and the Second Coming, was seized upon by Spanish chroniclers and soon became firmly entrenched in Conquest narratives.

Scholars of Nahuatl and of the Aztec culture of reverential or polite speech, agree that Moctezuma's speech reads as a regal and gracious welcome, not a surrender. Whether Cortés simply misunderstood—via his interpreters—or deliberately twisted the words of the emperor is not clear. But his interpretation made sound political sense. It was a report written to the king at a moment in the two-year war when the invasion was faltering; to depict the meeting with the emperor as a surrender that was reminiscent of the Muslim surrender of Granada to the Spanish king in 1492, despite the fact that Cortés had been violently expelled from the Aztec capital and half his men slaughtered, was pure spin.

But it was not just Cortés' political instincts and the jingoism of subsequent Spanish writers that cemented the tale of Moctezuma's surrender. Before long, another group of Spaniards—the Franciscans in Mexico—began to promote the notion that Cortés was a divine agent, God's medium for bringing the faith to Mexico. "Through this captain, God opened the door for us to preach his holy gospel," one of the Twelve, Motolinía (his name was taken from the Nahuatl for "poverty"), told the king. "Who has loved and defended the Indians of this new world like Cortés?" Motolinía was one of the first to spread the story that Indigenous Mexicans called the Spanish invaders gods, later adding the detail that Cortés was taken for Quetzalcoatl; it showed that the Mexicans had anticipated the Spaniards, hoping for their arrival in some sense, and that the Conquest was thus part of God's plan for the world.

The Nahuatl text quoted above, taken from the Florentine Codex, was itself influenced in various ways by the Franciscan millenarian vision of the Conquest, including the privileged role of Cortés within that narrative. The codex was the life's work of another early Franciscan in Mexico, Bernardino de Sahagún. He arrived in 1529 and worked on the project's twelve bilingual (Spanish-Nahuatl) volumes from 1547 into the 1580s. In 1579, he supervised the composition of the Nahuatl account of the Conquest but rewrote it five years later to greater magnify and glorify Cortés' providential role.

Viewed from either perspective—the Nahua account or the Franciscan one—Cortés comes off well and Moctezuma poorly. This is partly because the Nahua version was composed by men from Tlatelolco, a neighborhood of the Aztec capital city of Tenochtitlán, one that was once a separate town and that held out the longest during the brutal siege of 1520–1521. Moctezuma was not a Tlatelolcan; decades after his death and the empire's demise, he became a convenient target for Tlatelolcans keen to explain defeat while saving community face. Thus, Moctezuma the nervous, hesitant, cowardly ruler, terrorized by omens and kowtowing to the Spaniards, is fully present in the Codex Durán (see figure 4.6, one of the original illustrations from the codex). Seeming to be true, simply by virtue of being the view of the vanquished, the portrait is a Tlatelolcan-Franciscan invention, deeply Christianized and infused with millenarian themes.

Even the omens that supposedly unnerved the emperor upon the eve of the invention were introduced by Motolinía in the 1540s. They seem Indigenous enough—a comet over the Mexican night sky, a temple bursts into flames, another hit by lightning, the water on Lake Texcoco boils, and a crane with a mirror on its head caught in the lake. Yet all have been traced back to three ancient Mediterranean sources (by Plutarch, Lucan, and Josephus), classical works taught in the College of Santa Cruz set up by Franciscans in Tlatelolco to educate young, Nahua noblemen. The original omens predicted the falls of Jerusalem and Rome; for Indigenous Tlatelolcans and Franciscan friars alike, pre-Conquest Tenochtitlán was an ill-fated New World Rome and Jerusalem. And as the omens acquired Aztec details and merged with local fables, they too acquired a veneer of authenticity.

As Cortés's legend took form and solidified, so did Moctezuma's role as scapegoat for the Aztec defeat take clearer shape—the flip side of

Figure 4.6. Moctezuma, from the Codex Durán or *The History of the Indies of New Spain*, 1581. (Image in the public domain.)

the same coin. That coin was minted by the Franciscans, keen to maintain their vision of the New World as an opportunity to create on earth a version of the "New Jerusalem" described in the Book of Revelation. As a result, the history of the Conquest of Mexico was revised and reimagined, and Aztec culture infused with the Franciscans' millenarian spirit, as symbolized by the ill treatment given to the emperor's reputation. The story of how that process played out among the Maya—who were themselves faced with Franciscan friars not long after Moctezuma's death—is the focus of the next chapter.

• 5 •

Apocalypto

The Millennium Comes to the Maya

> A great and wondrous sign appeared in heaven: a woman clothed with the sun, with the moon under her feet and a crown of twelve stars on her head.
>
> —Book of Revelation 12:1

> Ask a devout Maya and he might answer in words which sound very much like a prophecy, "The Cross sleeps." And as the reader knows, that which sleeps might also awaken.
>
> —from the prologue to Hubert Smith's 2009 novel, *Maya Apocalypse: A Nelson Cocom Thriller*

> These characters have to be utterly believable as pre-Columbian Mesoamericans.
>
> —Mel Gibson, on the Maya protagonists of his 2006 movie, *Apocalypto*

In 1549, at the young age of twenty-five, Diego de Landa set out on an adventure that would define the rest of his life. Having become a Franciscan friar eight years earlier in Spain, he joined a new expedition of three other young priests sailing for the New World. Their mission was to assist their order's Catholic conversion of the Indigenous population of the Americas. Led by an older Franciscan friar named Lorenzo de Bienvenida, Landa was sent to the province of Yucatan. This small colony, in the northwest of the peninsula of that name, was considered perilous and challenging; the province's capital of Merida had only been founded seven years earlier, the dust was still settling after twenty years of invasion warfare and colonial rule, outside a few Spanish towns, had yet to be firmly established.

The two priests, Landa and Bienvenida, were assigned to missionize in the Chel region of the peninsula—east of Merida in a former kingdom where most of the local people had yet to see a Spanish priest, let alone be converted to Christianity. They were expected to establish a mission town at an appropriate locale, a base from which to spread the word.

After traveling through the region for several months, the duo came upon the ancient Maya metropolis of Itzmal (destined to become the colonial and modern town of Izamal). Although the town's population was a fraction of what it had been a thousand years earlier, and many of its older structures lay in ruins, Itzmal was still inhabited and—most importantly—still functioned as a major religious pilgrimage site. At its peak in early Classic times, Itzmal had been a monumental city, consisting of numerous vast pyramids, sparkling paved plazas, and large-scale

Figure 5.1. Frederick Catherwood, *Ruins at Izamal*, from the book *Incidents of Travel in Yucatan*, 1843. (Image in the public domain.)

public artwork (seen in figure 5.1, a nineteenth-century lithograph of a stucco sculpture that once decorated the side of a building). Straight, raised, white roads (called *sacbeob*) still linked the town to other important sites in the peninsula, such as neighboring Aké.

The chief object of the pilgrimages to the pyramids of the town was the Indigenous deity Itzamnaaj, the god of sacred knowledge and healing. Inspired by the sacred heritage of the town, Bienvenida and Landa began construction of a monumental church and monastery, erecting a Christian building directly on top of the Maya pyramid known to have originally housed Maya priests dedicated to the Itzamnaaj cult. Over the course of the next two decades, the church complex became the most elaborate in the province, eventually situating itself as the "jewel" of the Franciscan evangelical campaign. The complex was positioned sixteen feet above plaza level on the base of the original pyramid (seen in figure 5.2). In its finished form (which it had reached by the mid-seventeenth century), the complex consisted of a barrel-vaulted nave church, two double-storied cloisters, and a one thousand-square-foot atrium (seen in figure 5.3). This scale was an impressive feat by any colonial standards but particularly so in the relatively poor province of Yucatan.

Figure 5.2. The precontact pyramidal base of the monastic complex of Izamal, Yucatan, Mexico. (Photograph by the authors.)

Figure 5.3. The atrium of the monastic complex, Izamal, Yucatan, Mexico. (Photograph by the authors.)

The church's success stemmed partly from the ingenuity of Landa himself. Recognizing the site's sacred importance to the Maya population, he installed a carved Virgin Mary in the church, which for all intents and purposes began to take on the religious roles held by Itzamnaaj in the previous centuries. She was a healing Virgin, acclaimed to have numinous powers, and within a matter of years was visited by thousands of pilgrims annually. Landa's foresight was clearly well-grounded; today, the Virgin of Izamal is the patron saint of the Yucatan Peninsula.

As part of the original building program, executed a decade or so after the church's completion in the 1560s, Maya artists painted a series of murals. In the small room that led from the open expanse of the atrium and into the semiprivate space of the cloister, local Indigenous artists completed a multicolor scene that wrapped around the small room's walls, reaching from floor to ceiling. The murals are now heavily deteriorated due to the province's humid climate, but the scenes have survived sufficiently to lend insight into the reasoning behind the heavy investment placed in the conversion campaign by the Franciscans in Mexico and Yucatan (indeed, by all the religious orders in the New

World—not just the Franciscans, but also the Dominicans, Augustinians, and later the Jesuits too).

On the north wall, a pastoral scene is apparent (figure 5.4). Franciscan friars, identifiable due to their long, brown robes and tonsured heads, mingle in a landscape reminiscent of the Yucatan itself, with its low-lying shrub forests. Among the priests, Maya neophytes themselves participate in the peaceful scene, wandering among the Franciscans, playing drums, collecting honey, and—perhaps most significantly—engaging in penitent rituals.

Across the small room, the murals on the facing wall are opposite in intention (figure 5.5). Here, the scene is not one of peaceful respite but instead is imbued with violence. Less legible than the north wall, the south wall still clearly depicts a troubled landscape. Red-skinned beings appear to beat objects with long poles. Like the idyllic scene across the room, this violent action seems to take place in the Yucatan, as similar trees have been included to give the audience a notion of place. It easily brings to mind the gruesome scenes, visited in the previous chapter, that decorate the walls of the open chapel at Actopan.

Figure 5.4. North wall mural of the Izamal monastery *portería*, sixteenth century. (Photograph and overdrawing by the authors.)

96   Chapter 5

Figure 5.5. South wall mural of the Izamal monastery *portería*, sixteenth century. (Photograph and overdrawing by the authors.)

While these oppositional scenes could easily be read as a "good Indian/bad Indian" cautionary tale, another part of the mural cycle hints at the real significance of the paintings. On the east wall—the wall that connects the pastoral and demon paintings—a doorway leads directly into the cloister. Here, placed right above the doorjamb, a diminutive image of the Virgin was painted (figure 5.6). She is small, but she cannot be missed: one must walk right beneath her to enter the cloister (only later would she be bypassed by pilgrims wishing to pay homage to the Virgin of Izamal in her private chapel located behind the church's nave and only accessible through the cloister); and one's attention is grabbed by the bright hues that the Maya artist no doubt deliberately selected. Painted in a traditional red and blue robe, and then set against a vibrant yellow orb, this was no neutral or ordinary painting of the Virgin Mary. The Maya artists, undoubtedly under the direction of Izamal's resident Franciscan priests, had painted the Virgin of the Apocalypse.

As discussed earlier, the Virgin of the Apocalypse references a section of the New Testament's Book of Revelation in which the Second Coming of Christ is prophesied. "A great and wondrous sign appeared in heaven," wrote John, in the passages that inspired Dürer's famous print series. As a sign of the impending Apocalypse, according to John's vision, there appeared "a woman clothed with the sun, with the moon

Figure 5.6. East wall mural of the Izamal monastery *portería*, sixteenth century. (Photograph and overdrawing by the authors.)

under her feet and a crown of twelve stars on her head." Placed in the context of the monumental Izamal monastery, and situated between the pastoral and devil murals, this small Virgin of the Apocalypse was far larger in import than her diminutive portrait suggests. She not only referenced the Doomsday warnings of Revelation, but she also provided justification for the entirety of the conversion campaigns launched in the New World. In short, the efforts of the friars were justified and urgent; the souls of the Maya had to be saved soon, so as to prepare for—or more, so as to hasten—the Second Coming of Christ, the accompanying Apocalypse, and the glorious millennium to follow.

Landa's personal zeal for this millennial task continued to mount. After a dozen years of proselytizing the Maya and supervising the transformation of Itzmal into Izamal, the Spanish friar was called away to Merida. There he was promoted to head or "provincial" of the Franciscans in Yucatan, and as such he soon heard rumors of recidivism in Maya villages; that is, efforts by local men to maintain traditional "pagan" rituals and practices after the community had supposedly been converted to Christianity. In the spring of 1562, two young Maya boys outside the town of Mani, the headquarters of the Franciscan evangelical campaign, accidentally came upon a cache of ceramic sculptures and human skulls collected in a cave. The youths immediately returned to the village and described their discovery to the local priest. He ordered the cached objects brought into the church's atrium and commanded the Maya who lived close to the cave to come to Mani for questioning. They quickly admitted to using the objects to petition the native deities for rain, confessing that this was still a common local practice.

The Franciscan response was to bring down on the Maya a virtual apocalypse; within months, Mani became the epicenter of a full-scale Inquisition, led by Landa himself. Surrounding villages were ordered to turn over sculptures of Maya deities (termed *ídolos* by the Catholic priests, classifying them as satanic superstition) and precontact, accordion-fold books. All items were burned in massive bonfires in Mani. Thousands of Maya were arrested and questioned under the threat of torture. Many were put to torment on the pulley and the *burro*, a wooden rack to which victims were tied. As many as two hundred died during the summer months, hundreds more were left permanently scarred or crippled, and dozens appear to have committed suicide to avoid the agonies of Inquisition interrogations.

For the Maya of Mani and neighboring towns, 1562 was an end-of-world date, the long summer a harrowing series of Judgment Days. Indeed, a famous modern representation of the 1562 Inquisition portrays it in Doomsday hues. The second floor of the Palacio de Gobierno, on the northern edge of Merida's colonial plaza, is decorated with a mural cycle detailing Yucatec history from the precontact to the modern eras. Viewed by thousands of local inhabitants, schoolchildren, and foreign tourists each year, these images have become paradigmatic of the province's defining historical moments, perhaps shaping public opinion more than any ancient, colonial, or modern textual source. In the scene that depicts that violent summer in Mani, Landa himself is depicted not as a beneficent protector of the Maya—as his writings, partly composed in Spain in the 1560s as part of his defense during the investigation into his 1562 Inquisition, would have us believe—but as an evil torturer (figure 5.7).

Apocalypto 99

Figure 5.7. Fernando Castro Pacheco, *Diego de Landa and the Mani Inquisition of 1562*, located in the Palacio de Gobierno, Merida, Yucatan, Mexico. (Photograph by the authors.)

A mostly monochromatic scene composed of oranges and greyscale, Landa inhabits a full third of the composition. Poised above a vast fire in which carved statues of Maya deities can be seen succumbing to the tall flames, he presides over a figurative "end of the world," as the events were surely understood by the Maya. The Franciscan seems to be of the flames himself, the ashes, as he holds the Bible in his right hand, the ultimate justification for the unmediated violence, and a burning pole in his left, proclaiming his ultimate culpability for this tragedy. His facial expression is stern and unmoving, providing modern viewers a transparent, if not, perhaps, overstated, understanding of his religious convictions.

~

These moments from the first dozen years of Spiritual Conquest in Yucatan—the missionary zeal of Landa, the murals and structures of Izamal, the apocalyptic summer of 1562—are vivid symbols of the millenarian determination of the Franciscans to convert the Maya. In the Maya world as a whole, that process proved to be a protracted and complex one—begun in the late 1520s in Guatemala and stretching across the centuries of colonial rule into the modern period. Just as conversion efforts in central Mexico resulted in local Nahua versions of Catholicism, so did Maya Catholicisms emerge in colonies in Yucatan and Guatemala.

A core feature of the local form of Catholicism forged in Yucatan by Franciscans and Maya neophytes was millennial ideology—not simply imposed upon or injected into the Maya worldview but appropriated by Maya elders, scribes, and religious officials. In chapter 1, we discussed the tale of the destruction of the world from the *Books of the Chilam Balam of Chumayel*, primarily using the passage that one translator named "the ceremonial of the *baktun*" and another "the creation of the world." Having deliberately presented this material in such a way as to emphasize the supposedly "pure" Indigenous apocalyptic nature of these texts, we now revisit them, placing them more fully within the historical and cultural context in which they were written and rewritten. Viewed as such, these passages tell a drastically different story, one in which Franciscan millennial ideology plays a far more prominent role than 2012ologists would have had us believe. These seemingly Maya passages are, in fact, directly channeled from medieval European preoccupations with the end of the world.

In a tragic irony of colonialism, the Spaniards who brought torture and slaughter, widespread enslavement, and waves of epidemic disease that reduced the Maya population by as much as 90 percent over several generations, also brought an ideology that helped Mayas understand what was happening to their world. More than imminent, the Apocalypse had already arrived.

One of the contributors to the Chumayel manuscript—a late seventeenth-century Maya scribe who goes unnamed—wrote into the book a twenty-page summary of Maya mythistory. This ranged from texts detailing the origins of the ancient gods to the creation of human beings and calendrical rituals of his own day (we quoted from it in chapter 1). Much of it was, no doubt, copied from earlier alphabetic versions of ancient glyphic texts, such as the Dresden Codex. But much of it was influenced by Christianity, directly drawn from sources brought to Yucatan by Franciscan friars.

The creation-of-the-world narrative is an example of this Maya blending of European material with local traditions. The reworking of the old Oxlahuntiku/Bolontiku myth so that it concludes with a Christian-style Apocalypse obviously made sense to the colonial-era Maya scribe. As we saw in chapter 1, the destruction of the world is presented as a cosmic battle between the deities associated with the celestial realm and the Underworld, Oxlahuntiku and Bolontiku. Bolontiku destroys Oxlahuntiku, heaping upon him a series of abuses until his rain god aspect is removed from the heavens. This sets the stage for a monumental flood that destroys—or will destroy—the world.

Immediately after Oxlahuntiku's destruction, however, the world flowers with a variety of edible plant species. This destruction/creation sequence, culminating in the flowering of the next era, parallels Maya agricultural techniques of slash and burn, whereby the naturally occurring flora of a *milpa* (cornfield) must be destroyed for more useful plants to be cultivated and flourish. After the mythic flowering, the corn plant is stolen away, resulting in the collapse of the world. Cosmic destruction is ushered in by the anticipated deluge. Whether read as "a rush of rain, one sharp burst of rain" (our translation) or "one fetching of rain, one lancing of rain" (as one Maya scholar has it), the phrase hints at the violence of the apocalyptic flood as it wipes out the "heartless people." The deities called the *bacabob* (the Bacabs) then reestablish the geographical limits of the world's terrestrial plane, setting up a colored tree in each of the four corners and in the center of the universe.

The details of the story have obvious precontact roots, and the agricultural metaphor is likewise highly localized. But the apocalyptic tone suggests the Book of Revelation, an impression confirmed by the passage that immediately follows. Here we defer to the translation by Timothy Knowlton (an anthropologist who specializes in colonial period Maya creation mythology):

> And thus the word of this *katun* may be accomplished / And then it was given by Dios / A deluge occurs for the second time / This is the destruction of the world / Then this ends / That Our Lord who is Jesus Christ may then descend / Upon the valley of Jehoshaphat beside the town of Jerusalem / It occurred that he redeems us by his holy blood.

The references to the Apocalypse and the Second Coming are explicit; but, do we know exactly how they made their way into Maya alphabetic writings composed far away from overseeing friars and for specifically Maya-only purposes? Knowlton has determined that two versions of a popular European account of apocalyptic lore were translated into Yucatec Mayan during the colonial period. This text, titled *Fifteen Signs before Doomsday*, appears in the *Books of the Chilam Balam* kept by the village of Tusik and in another Maya text that scholars call the Morley Manuscript (a little-studied text that is akin to a *Chilam Balam* book). Of these fifteen signs, the first is a global flood that leads to the Last Judgment.

Of particular relevance to our argument here is the fact that the prophesy of the Second Coming of Christ is the climax to these Maya passages. This was not inserted to mollify Spanish priests; Europeans were never intended to see the highly guarded, clandestine books written by and exclusively for Maya authors and readers. In fact, the Maya of Chumayel, Tusik, and other villages could safely assume that if a Franciscan happened to stumble upon the manuscript, they would have destroyed it; the friars continued to burn suspect texts of Maya authorship for some two hundred years after Landa's great Inquisition bonfire of 1562. So how then can these explicit references to Christianity be explained? We cannot assume that they were afterthoughts merely tacked on to the end of an otherwise purely Maya creation story because they were deemed "interesting" or perhaps "innovative" to the Maya authors.

On the contrary, Christian passages and ideas permeate the entire *Chilam Balam* text. For example, the flood and subsequent creation of the world is itself presided over by a Christian, not Maya, protagonist. This is not made clear in the classic translation of the passage by the late Ralph Roys: "There would be a sudden rush of water when the theft of the insignia [of Oxlahuntiku] occurred. Then the sky would fall, it would fall down upon the earth, when the four gods, the four Bacabs, were set up, who brought about the destruction of the world." However, the supposedly Mayan word that Roys translated as "insignia"—*cangel*—is in other Maya documents used as a version of "Archangel." The difference may seem small—a case of Mayanists arguing over minutiae—but it actually transforms the passage into a highly hybridized account of creation in which, directly following the Flood, the Archangel of the cornfield arrives to oversee the setting up of the new creation.

Dissatisfied with Roys's version, a later scholar, the late Munro Edmonson, reinterpreted the Oxlahuntiku creation story as a passage about the calendar. The result was a kind of chain reaction that resulted in a further misrepresentation used to support the supposed 2012 evidence found in colonial Maya sources. In chapter 1, we quoted Edmonson's translation and comments on the "millennial words" that marked the celebration in Merida of the *baktun* ending in 1618. The impression that Edmonson gives, and which we deliberately echoed, is that as recently as the start of the current *baktun*—which ended in December 2012—the Maya were still ritually celebrating the four-hundred-year cycle; indeed, he states bluntly that the Long Count lasted this late. In the decades since Edmonson translated the *Chilam Balam of Chumayel*, this impression has been cited numerous times and has worked its way into the fabric of Maya calendar studies and 2012ology.

It is, however, misleading. The passage does *not* record a Long Count date, nor is there any evidence in this or any of the *Chilam Balam* books that the Maya were still maintaining the Long Count of Classic times. The passage does not describe a *baktun*, or ever use the term; the book refers only to the *tun* (the solar year) and the twenty-year cycle of the *katun*. It was Edmonson himself, not the Maya authors, who dubbed the passage *The Ceremonial of the Baktun*; in the original manuscript, it has no title, unless one counts the title on the previous page, *Quinto: 1620* (*Fifth: 1620*). Edmonson dismisses this, unconvincingly, as "a late addition," but close examination of the handwritings reveals it to have been written by the same person (see figure 5.8). The passage in fact describes the ritual ending of a *katun* cycle, but because that cycle happened to be the final one in a *baktun*, Edmonson inferred (in effect, invented) the larger "ceremony."

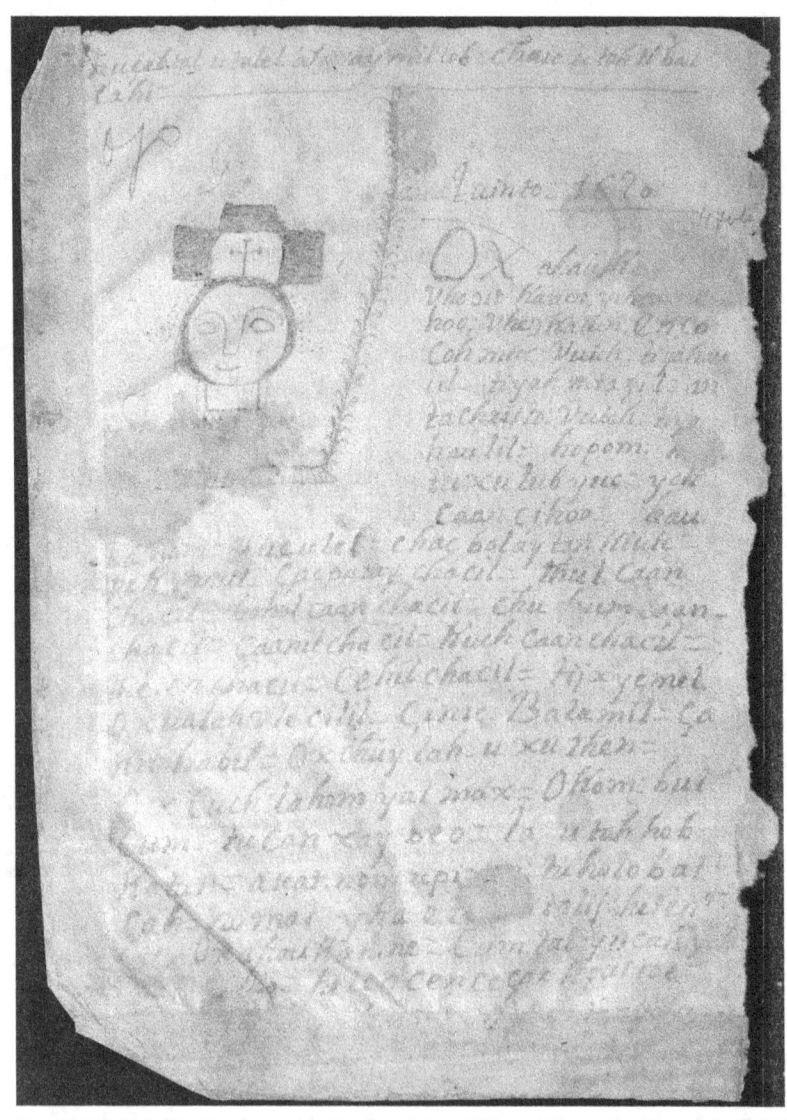

Figure 5.8. Folio 49v from the *Books of the Chilam Balam of Chumayel*. (Held by the Princeton University Library, Mesoamerican Manuscripts no. 4; image in the public domain.)

As for the text itself, it is heavily imbued with the influences of Christian and Spanish culture. One of the officials at the ritual is described as being the *Antachristo* (the Antichrist, representing the Maya who refuse to convert to Christianity), and the presiding officer claims to be called Ceçar Agusto (Caesar Augustus). There is no corroborating evidence to prove these ceremonies actually took place in Merida in 1618 or 1620. But assuming they did, they represented a stage in the centuries-long process whereby the rituals that marked the old Maya calendar were reconciled to the rituals of the Christian calendar. The result in modern times (that is, roughly the past century and a half) is a hybrid set of rituals. Some of these have clear ancient Maya roots (like the Chachac ceremony marking the onset of the rains; Chac is an old rain god), some look like old rituals heavily colonized by Christianity (Good Friday replacing the earlier rites of ritual execution).

How does it relate to 2012ology? There are three key points regarding this *Chilam Balam* source. First, it is a speculative stretch to read it as being focused on the celebration of a *baktun* cycle, as representing ongoing Maya concerns with a calendar marked by beginnings and endings in 1224, 1618, and 2012. Second, to interpret the language as "millennial" is to add an implication of specific apocalyptic awareness and expectation—not just a knowledge of Second Coming ideology but a timetable for it—that is not in the original text. Third, while we can detect ancient Maya and early modern Christian elements in the passage, it is ultimately best understood as colonial-period Maya literature, written by people who saw their culture not as piecemeal, a patchwork of two contributing cultures, but as something singular, coherent, traditional, and local—as theirs.

Why did the Maya intellectuals in the colonial period intentionally incorporate Christian theologies into their cosmologies by choice? And more specifically, why were Christian accounts of the Apocalypse so appealing to these Maya authors, when for thousands of years a nonmillennial creation mythology had successfully served the needs of the Maya culture? As Knowlton has stated, "The Christian apocalypse made sense to Colonial Maya scribes within the context of an otherwise Postclassic mythic narrative itself." In other words, when Christianity was introduced to the Yucatec Maya, they intentionally adopted aspects that could most easily be dovetailed into their preexisting worldview. The mixing of the two contributing ideologies resulted in a third cultural system, completely independent of the original two.

Recall that ancient Mesoamerican cultures conceived of time as largely cyclical, divided and charted in a series of interlocking cycles of varying lengths. They also saw creation and re-creation as a continual cycle, with previous worlds stretching out behind our own current lived reality, as having occurred three or four times previously. With this as a starting point, it is easy to see how Christian accounts of the Apocalypse, with the Second Coming of Christ and the creation of a new world, would have made a "New Jerusalem" appealing to a Maya audience. In the new reality of their colonial world—many thousands of Indigenous peoples felled by disease, tried and punished for their religious beliefs, forcibly removed from land they had inhabited for centuries—there must have been some kind of comfort in finding links between their traditional worldviews and those being forced upon them by Catholic priests. The incorporation of Christian themes was not necessarily a succumbing to colonial forces; it can also be seen as a socially savvy way to maintain cultural continuity amid the psychological trauma of the early colonial period. Apocalyptic narratives and their associated millennial theology were an ideal avenue through which converted Maya could make sense of the violence and cultural upheavals of the Spanish conquest and its chaotic aftermath.

The colonial Maya literature of the *Books of Chilam Balam* thus tells us much about Maya history and culture; but it does not support the notion that the Maya anticipated 2012 with any sort of anxiety, if at all, either before the Spanish invasion or after. On the contrary, it shows how Spanish-Franciscan views of Christianity influenced the Maya intellectual landscape, infusing some European millenarian concerns into their Indigenous perception of creation and time.

∽

What happened to this imported Maya millenarian tradition? As a product of the colonial encounter of the sixteenth century, did it survive the centuries that followed, including the early nineteenth, when Yucatan ceased to be a Spanish colony? And if it did not die out, is there a thread of continuity through to Maya-based 2012ology?

As it turned out, Maya millenarianism *did* survive throughout the colonial period and into the nineteenth century (when Yucatan became part of the Mexican republic), and it manifested itself in a way that was vibrant, violent, and distinct to the Maya of the Yucatan. In ways that would have shocked the Franciscans of earlier centuries, the millenarian ideas they had introduced came to the fore within the context of the peninsula's prolonged nineteenth-century civil conflict dubbed the Caste War. Although the war began in 1847 as a political and regional struggle, with Hispanic and Maya protagonists on both sides, it soon evolved into a kind of race war. Most fascinatingly—and most significantly for our story—one group of Maya rebels maintained an independent state in the east into the twentieth century, ruled by a religious-political government that became known as the Cult of the Talking Cross.

Let us step back again into the colonial centuries for a moment. While the northwest section of the peninsula had been heavily influenced by a strong Spanish presence since the earliest days of contact in the sixteenth century, the eastern half of the peninsula remained largely uncolonized for three hundred years. Brief forays were made into this region by Franciscans and other Spaniards—motivated primarily by commercial interests—but, for the most part, the Maya maintained a fairly traditional way of life. Spanish maps called the region *despoblado* (uninhabited), which of course it was not. A major Spanish conquest expedition against independent Maya in the 1690s largely bypassed the kingdoms of the east in order to destroy the larger Itza Maya kingdom in the Peten region of northern Guatemala.

This is not to say that the Maya of the peninsula's southeast (its east, the Peten, and Belize) were not impacted by Franciscan ideologies or by Spanish colonization. On the contrary, they undoubtedly were, but unlike Maya communities to the north and west, the Mayas of the southeast were entirely or largely independent—and free to incorporate specific aspects of the new religion into their traditional worldview on their own terms. The entire culture of the eastern villages of the peninsula might be likened to the self-conscious appropriations of relevant biblical material into the clandestine, Maya-authored *Books of the Chilam Balam* discussed earlier. Meanwhile, Maya leaders in cities like Lamanai, in what is today Belize, maintained a local form of Christianity for generations after Franciscan friars had left. We cannot know for sure how infused with millenarian thinking Maya Christianity in Belize was, but there were likely efforts to reconcile Franciscan apocalypticism with local Maya mythology and ideology—as there was both within the Spanish colony of Yucatan and in the independent kingdom in the Peten. Indeed, despite the tendency by scholars of the Itza kingdom to see the history and culture of Maya prophecy as a causal factor in its defeat in 1697, it seems very clear—both from the larger context outlined here and from the specifics of Franciscan expeditions into the Peten throughout the seventeenth century—that the prophetic tradition of the Itza was yet another example of how Mayas accommodated or appropriated Franciscan millenarian ideas in order to help make sense of the disruptive, often disastrous, presence of Spaniards in the Maya world.

Meanwhile, within the Spanish colony of northern Yucatan, the persistence of nativist millenarian thought was revealed starkly in 1761, when a disaffected Maya villager named Jacinto Uc declared himself to be a returning, liberating king. He was, he claimed, not only an envoy and manifestation of Christ, but was also both a returning Canek (the last king of the Itza Maya of the Peten) and a returning Montezuma (a deft reversal of the myth, invented by Franciscans two centuries earlier, that Moctezuma had surrendered to Cortés because he took him for a returning deified Indigenous king). The uprising was short-lived and localized, crushed with extreme violence by Spanish officials; Jacinto Canek King Moctezuma received his own apocalyptic ending, tortured slowly to death in Merida's central plaza. But he had persuaded a significant number of the region's Maya leaders and villagers of the efficacy of his vision of a new millennium—one free of Spanish colonists but loyal to the Virgin Mary, to be ruled by a regime totally Maya but more resolutely Christian than the one he sought to overthrow.

The Maya transformation of Franciscan millenarianism into something autochthonous and nativist was thus deep-rooted, and it continued after the wars that led to Mexican independence from Spain. In the wake of Independence, problems began to arise across the Yucatan Peninsula. Regional rivalries, political factionalism within the ruling Hispanic elite, disputes over whether Yucatan should be part of the Mexican republic or an independent nation—these conflicts ensnared attempts by Maya elders to protect communal lands from private incursion. What ensued was a complex half-century of sporadic warfare that pitted the underprivileged Maya population against the powerful Hispanic elite. While the fight may have begun as a messy political endeavor, it was soon transformed into a social and racial war that eventually took on religious dimensions.

Early on in the war's history, in 1850, the Maya leaders of the rebel movement in the east established a new headquarters at a *cenote* (a natural sinkhole) called Chan Santa Cruz, Little Sacred Cross. Near the cave a large mahogany tree grew, upon which was carved an image of a cross, lending the site its name. A native religious cult emerged centered on veneration of this cross, quickly gaining support among the Indigenous rebels. A sanctuary was built nearby to house the religious icon referred to as X-Balam Na, the Jaguar House, now largely destroyed.

Shortly after the Jaguar House was built, the cross began to "speak" to the local Maya. Historical records later revealed that the Cross had several interpreters who voiced the Cross's concerns and petitions. This Talking Cross soon became highly influential. It urged the Maya not to end their battle with the Spanish population, "Because it has come / The time / For an Indian Uprising / Over the Whites / Once and for all." Through his interpreters, the Talking Cross offered God's protection, even promising them invincibility in battle. The cult's followers were called the Cruzob (the Spanish for "cross" with a Mayan plural, *-ob*).

Despite the power of the Talking Cross, many Cruzob rebels lost their lives in the attacks and skirmishes that followed. The Hispanic state's mixed-race army then moved in on Chan Santa Cruz, stealing the Cross and killing one of its interpreters, a rebel leader named Manuel Nauat. But millenarian belief tends to be remarkably resistant to disappointment, and this was as much the case in nineteenth-century Yucatan as it was elsewhere. The rebel Maya simply installed a new Cross to replace the confiscated original, with the new one communicating in writing via the assistance of a handful of scribes. There were also a group of smaller, proxy crosses, carried into battle for divine protection. Like the Talking Cross, the proxies tended to be draped in an *ipil* (or *huipil*), the traditional garment worn by Maya women. This was a Christian cross, its symbolic power derived from the faith introduced three centuries earlier by Franciscans; but the cult had a distinctly Maya identity, forged by Maya to serve a local movement, the cause of the Cruzob.

Eventually, the strife faded and fizzled out. In 1901, the Mexican army advanced again on Chan Santa Cruz, taking it without a fight, occupying it and the surrounding Maya villages. The international border to the south, between Mexico and Belize, had been formalized in the previous decade, eventually resulting in the creation of a new Mexican state, Quintana Roo. But resentments, hostilities, and even millenarian expectations persisted. The eastern half of the Yucatan Peninsula remained relatively dangerous for non-Maya peoples well into the twentieth century—the last recognized skirmish was recorded in 1933, giving the Caste War a total span of some eighty-five years. As late as the 1960s, Maya elders in the east expressed an expectation that an outsider would bring guns and encourage the Cruzob to rise up again.

And today? What has become of this seemingly isolated outpost of the Spanish Empire? Has the Cruzob cause seized upon the imminence of 2012 and emerged again to prepare the Maya for apocalypse and renewal? Are there any direct lines of influence and ideology between the ancient Maya of the Long Count, the Cruzob Maya of eastern Yucatan, and the 2012 phenomenon?

In short, no; there is no such direct line. Instead, the lines of influence run from medieval Christianity to colonial and Caste War–era Yucatan, and parallel (not in series) to that same medieval source for the modern phenomenon of interpreting the ancient Long Count to serve 2012ology. Ironically, the eastern coast of the peninsula has witnessed a Maya resurgence, but hardly the kind imagined by Cruzob elders. While the ancient Maya were appropriated by 2012ologists (admittedly, in a spirit of profound appreciation), international and Mexican business interests appropriated the ancient Maya (in a spirit of exploitation) in order to dramatically refigure the east into a tourist zone. They named it the "Riviera Maya."

Centered around the modern development of Isla Cancún (as opposed to colonial Cancún, located a few miles inland), a largely North American and European tourist base can enjoy the natural splendor of the Yucatan's east coast at scores of hotels and eco-resorts. For those visitors willing to take a break from suntanning, snorkeling, zip lining, and wet T-shirt contests, numerous agencies are set up to bring curious tourists on trips farther south and inland to fully restored ancient Maya sites. The most accessible are Chichén Itzá and Tulum, but the efforts of archaeologists and road crews have gradually been putting more cities in range for decades. At the time of writing, there are ongoing plans for a tourism train line to link vacationers on the eastern coast to archaeological sites as far away as Palenque, Calakmul, and the capital of Merida.

The 2012 phenomenon was expected to give such tourism a boost, and it did to some extent; that is, visitor totals increased around and after 2012, but the larger context was an explosion in tourism in Cancún and the Riviera Maya from the late 1990s (when annual numbers crossed the half-million line) to the late 2010s (when they reached between seven and eight million, with an additional four million cruise ship passengers stopping at the island of Cozumel). But while it is unlikely that 2012ology inspired many of those millions to choose Yucatan, it did have an impact on specialty tourism; in particular, in the years leading up to and including 2012, various end-of-world celebrations and expeditions took place. One of these—a further twist of irony, in view of the argument laid out in this chapter—was an event called The Prophets Conference: 2012 Tipping Point, which took place in Cancún at the start of 2010. The speakers, or "faculty," were prominent modern Gnostics and New Age 2012ologists who saw 2012 as marking "a new birth of human consciousness" (Graham Hancock), "the beginning of a new cycle into an expanded planetary being" (Cody Johnson), "a return of the feminine" (Christine Page), and an "apocalyptic passage" through which "we will conceive ourselves, increasingly, as fractal expressions of a unified field of consciousness and sentient aspects of a planetary ecology" (Graham Pinchbeck).

"The purpose of the Maya coming to this planet was very specific," proclaimed José Argüelles on The Prophets Conference website, "to leave behind a definite set of clues and information about the nature and purpose of our planet at this particular time in the solar system and in the galactic field." As he died in 2011, Argüelles did not live to see the end of 2012 bring "a brilliant explosion of knowledge" (let alone the return of the extraterrestrial ancient Maya). But, over a decade later, his words were still live on the conference website—as were the more measured phrases of the late John Major Jenkins, for whom the meeting of 2012ologists was "to explore a radically different, more optimistic interpretation of the Mayan prophecy—as referring to the end of the world as we have known it." How the 2012 phenomenon got to this (tipping) point—considering the ancient Maya roots and medieval Christian sources detailed in the previous chapters—is the subject of our final chapter.

· 6 ·

We Are Always Almost There

Why People Believe

It may end later, but I see no reason for its ending sooner. This I mention not to assert when the time of the end shall be, but to put a stop to the rash conjectures of fancifull men who are frequently predicting the time of the end, and by doing so bring the sacred prophesies into discredit as often as their predictions fail.

—Sir Isaac Newton, predicting in 1705 that the world would end on or after 2060

Five years, that's all we've got.

—David Bowie, 1972

Events in history are no accident.

—prophecy popularizer Salem Kirban's 1989 pamphlet and cassette *The Great Conspiracy*

To learn much more about the details of the end of the world, you are invited to write Family Radio . . . I Hope God Will Save Me! We Are Almost There!"

—2008 pamphlet distributed nationally by Family Radio, based in Oakland, California

Deep in the Maya rain forests, near the border between Belize and Guatemala, is a small hotel—a "jungle lodge" bed and breakfast called Sweet Songs. Spectacular Maya cities like Tikal are a few hours' drive away, so the lodge thrives on ancient ruins tourism. For several years leading up to the week of December 18–22, 2012, Sweet Songs (then called duPlooy's, after the family who had founded it in 1988) offered a five-day "Apocalypto" special, complete with tours of nearby Maya sites. And there was a Doomsday twist. If the lodge—and the world—still existed on the fifth night, that of December 22, your stay that night was free. "If you think that we will still be here," proclaimed the lodge's website, "this is a bargain. If you don't, at least you won't have to pay for the 22nd!"

You are probably smiling at this. So too, no doubt, were the owners of duPlooy's Jungle Lodge and of other hotels within range of Tikal, as their reservation books filled. So too must have the Apocalypto tourists smiled over their jungle breakfasts on December 22—apocalyptic hangovers aside. In the end—or rather, after the end—2012 was a smiling matter.

But it was also a seriously widespread phenomenon, a magnet for worldwide weirdness that took on industrial proportions. Indeed, the very extent of the 2012 phenomenon was arguably its most significant feature. Those interested in booking the Apocalypto special at duPlooy's could have prepared for the trip by choosing among hundreds of books on 2012 predictions available in the 2000s. Some of those publications sought to explain the phenomenon in a serious way, and many successfully debunked the myths of 2012 based on misinterpretations of astronomical patterns or of the Maya calendar. But most of the literature was built upon sensationalizing the idea that *something* would happen in 2012. "Prophecy," "destiny," "catastrophe," "apocalypse," "extinction," "secret," "mystery," and yes, "the end of the world"—these were the terms that adorned the titles of such books. There were thousands of 2012 websites too. In fact, if one includes websites not devoted entirely to the phenomenon but containing chatter about it, the number rose to tens of millions; most have yet to be taken down.

The ultimate and, perhaps, most important question, then, is not whether the world ended in 2012 (it did not, as much as world events since then have sometimes seemed nightmarish or unreal); or whether the prophecies were off by a few years and the end is still nigh (we doubt that, but nobody knows for sure); or whether the Maya predicted the end would come in 2012 or sometime soon (they did not); or how millenarian ideas permeated the Maya world (Franciscan friars brought them from Europe); or what civilization most nurtured notions of the

Apocalypse (it was Western, not Mesoamerican). The final question is, why were people so quick to believe in 2012—and continue to be anxious about the Apocalypse, even when 2012 proved to be yet another Great Disappointment?

∼

Let us tackle this question by starting at the outer edges of the problem, with the more general question of why people believe in things *like* 2012; we shall then move inward toward the Western millenarian tradition, before ending where we began, with the Maya.

The belief in things *like* 2012, whether we call it belief in pseudoscience or "weird things," might be placed in two intertwined categories that are also relevant specifically to millenarianism and to 2012 speculation—optimistic and pessimistic.

"More than any other, the reason people believe weird things is because they want to," remarks Michael Shermer, a prolific writer on pseudoscience and the "borderlands" of belief ("where sense meets nonsense," as the title of one of his books puts it). Belief in weird things is "comforting" and "consoling"; it offers "immediate gratification." In other words, people believe in psychics and ghosts, UFOs and alien abductions, Atlantis and channeling, and the imminence of the Apocalypse or a new age for the same reason that people embrace religious faith. Belief offers an explanation without need for evidence. It offers a simple solution to life's complexities, a source of meaning and hope in a world of cruel whimsy and chaos.

A similar argument, put bluntly and less charitably, is that people are ignorant. A lack of education or understanding of the complexities of the Maya calendar, of the history of millenarianism in the West, or of the movements of the planets makes all of us vulnerable to overly simplistic, pseudoscientific predictions. Without the specialist knowledge that 99.9 percent of the population cannot possibly acquire, it can be hard to distinguish between science and pseudoscience, evidence and faith: Are evolution and global warming real? Can happy thoughts really produce happy molecules? Can dates like Y2K and 2012 really be preordained as terminal? That confusion and vulnerability has for many centuries been exploited by self-proclaimed messiahs, gurus, and cult leaders of all kinds—not to mention the racists who promote Holocaust denial, the fundamentalists who spread creationism, and the politicians who scoff at climate change. Not believing can be lonely. Embracing a position, taking a leap of faith, as nonsensical or "weird" as the belief may at first seem, can bring the comfort of belonging to a group, the reassurance of a shared belief and a common identity.

Religion and popular culture scholar Douglas Cowan has observed that the popular anticipation of the end-times imagines multiple possible outcomes, variously combining our millennial dreams (what we call here optimistic beliefs) and our apocalyptic nightmares (pessimistic beliefs). But all are underpinned by three shared understandings: that "human life is fragile"; and "human technology is fickle"; yet "the human spirit is strong," even "indomitable." As abstract as those three principles may seem, they are ubiquitous in popular culture, manifested in innumerable creative products in film, print, game, and every other medium.

For example, the most successful movie franchise of all time—a $20-billion enterprise of twenty-five films now entering its seventh decade—is predicated on those same three assumptions. In the James Bond universe—permeated with apocalyptic anxiety, secret knowledge, deadly conspiracies at the highest levels, and a highly conflicted attitude toward technology—humanity is unceasingly vulnerable to the misuse of scientific knowledge, personified by a conspiratorial, Antichrist-like archvillain, hell-bent on Doomsday. But the human spirit always triumphs, personified by the indomitable flawed Christ that is 007, ready to repeatedly sacrifice himself to save the world at the last minute—sometimes the last second. Being brought to the brink of extinction with every film is a thrill because we believe in Bond—ageless, immortal, and (as one actor after another takes on the role) endlessly replaceable—just as we believe that someone will always save *our* world, that somehow the latest looming cataclysm will be averted.

The optimistic and pessimistic beliefs are therefore like the two halves of a seesaw. With respect to 2012, the fear that the world was coming to a catastrophic end that December 21 (the pessimistic half of the mania) was balanced by the belief that the "end" was really the start of a new era of hope and enlightenment (the optimistic half). The two halves are connected, needing each other to exist. The millions of people worldwide who encountered 2012 ideas were able to move up and down the seesaw, finding confirmation for their pessimism about the world or reassurance that there was a future—perhaps a better one—beyond December 21.

This flexibility of form (which political scientist Michael Barkun calls "improvisational millennialism")—with optimism and pessimism on the same spectrum—has long been elemental to millenarianism in the West, apparent before and since 2012, applicable to any prophesied date. The pessimistic dwells on the end; think of it as the Four Horsemen trampling on humankind or massive earthquakes swallowing Las Vegas and Los Angeles. The optimistic is more properly called chiliasm or millennialism. As we saw in previous chapters, the Christian version holds that Christ will return again, ushering in a Paradise on Earth for a thousand years (*millennial*-ism) before the Final Judgment. The nondenominational version sees the present as flawed, even disastrous, but anticipates history moving teleologically or progressively toward an ideal future. That future is sometimes based on the return of an imagined Golden Age of long ago.

Chiliasm is at the very heart of modern Western civilization, so much so that we are not even aware of it as such. It is not just manifest in more obvious ways, such as the gamut of Christian churches from Pentecostal Protestantism to Seventh-day Adventism to Marian Catholicism. It is also built into Marxism and free-market capitalism. Those two ideologies are rightly seen as being in opposition to each other. Yet both base their legitimacy on a claim to be the only way society can progress toward utopia, be it through class struggle, with communism as the utopian goal, or through market freedom with universal individual prosperity as the goal. Chiliastic impulses have always underpinned and driven the trajectory of the history of the United States, from evangelical fundamentalism to libertarianism, from Manifest Destiny to modern notions of American exceptionalism, from revitalization movements to 2012ology and beyond.

In his classic study of what he called the "revolutionary millenarianism" of the Middle Ages, Norman Cohn stressed that the "aims and premises" of millenarian social movements were "boundless." Lacking the "specific, limited objectives" of other movements, they viewed themselves as uniquely important, built on the anticipation of "a cataclysm from which the world is to emerge totally transformed." What strikes us about Cohn's emphasis on boundlessness is how closely it describes modern millenarianism, with its improvisational capacity to borrow premises and pieces, fact-fiction reversals and imaginary codes, from a dizzying array of sources. Today's bricolage millenarianism is both a direct heir to medieval movements and at the same time something very modern (dare we say postmodern) in its ecumenical ubiquity. It both threatens appalling (world-ending) violence and also seems utterly harmless; it takes itself deadly serious, yet it is also the stuff of cartoons, action-movie franchises, escapist TV shows, and tourist T-shirts.

The eschatological and millenarian threads run so deeply and colorfully through our civilization that the Apocalypse is a casual, quotidian reference point—deployed for alarmist purposes, as with the more hysterical Y2K and 2012 literature, or as the butt of parody, as each passing end-date tends to become. The British magazine *The End Is Nigh* was thus a successful concept because its references were familiar (figure 6.1 is the cover of volume 3). Few readers, especially outside Britain, may know the precise origins of the sandwich-board Doomsday prophet (he walked up and down London's Oxford Street in the 1960s and 1970s, although his precursors go all the way back to Victorian days). But most will recognize him as an icon of contemporary apocalyptic anxiety. We are so accustomed to being warned that the end is imminent that phrases such as "The alien threat among us!" "Asteroids could wipe us out!" and "The Official Magazine of the Apocalypse!" are as funny as *The End Is Nigh* intended them to be.

Indeed, the movie *2012* was a hit because it worked as a lightweight, not ponderous, spectacle. Vast cities crumbled, hundreds of millions of people died, one protagonist after another suffered the loss of family members and then they themselves perished. Yet the makers of the film were able to draw on a fundamentally funny undercurrent to end-of-world fears so as to parody previous disaster flicks (including director Roland Emmerich's own). Audiences laughed not just because the film was (arguably) bad, or because it did not take itself too seriously, but because the end of the world has become a potentially humorous subject. As *New York Times* film reviewer Manohla Dargis succinctly states, *2012* is "Old Testament-style destruction served with a smile."

When in 1938 Orson Welles narrated an adaptation of H. G. Wells's *The War of the Worlds* on CBS radio, set in part as a series of news bulletins covering a Martian invasion, some audiences famously took it to be an actual news broadcast. "Radio Listeners in Panic," ran a front-page *New York Times* headline the next day. "A wave of mass hysteria

Figure 6.1. Oliver Redding, "The End Is Nigh," cover for *The Official Magazine of the Apocalypse*, vol. 3 (summer 2006). (Collection of the authors.)

seized thousands of radio listeners," the newspaper reported, when the broadcast "led thousands to believe that an interplanetary conflict had started with invading Martians spreading wide death and destruction in New Jersey and New York." The article went on to describe some of the 875 calls that were received by the *Times*'s own switchboard. A man from Dayton, Ohio, for example, called the newspaper desk to enquire at "what time will it be the end of the world?" Later the same evening a woman visited a New York police station with her two young children and extra clothing in tow. She planned to leave town, but New York's finest were able to convince her to stay.

A subsequent study of the panic concluded that more than a million terrified listeners took the broadcast literally. Today, we laugh and marvel at such public gullibility. But laughter can be a way to hide discomfort. Douglas Cowan has argued that the *War of the Worlds* broadcast was a milestone moment in the modern fusing of "apocalyptic imagination and popular culture"; "we have not looked at the permanence of our world the same way since." By the 1930s, Americans had already been primed by radio and print culture (see figure 6.2) to be both entertained and apprehensive, amused by and afraid of the myriad ways in which the world could suddenly end. Over the century that ensued, that paradoxical response to Doomsday has become global and increasingly multifaceted. It might seem as if we simply went from taking *The War of the Worlds* seriously to loving 007 and laughing at *2012*. But the proliferation of movies, TV shows, books, video games, televangelists, websites, and every conceivable media outlet for communicating endtimes fears, ideas, and entertainment has been paralleled by very real scares. By bringing death and suffering yet failing to end the world, scares such as the Cold War's nuclear holocaust, outbreaks of terrorism, the extreme weather of climate change, and the COVID-19 pandemic, helped foment that bifurcation of response. Genuine and widespread fear is constantly fed, while a kind of amused malaise is simultaneously maintained by each passing apocalyptic false alarm.

Western civilization's tradition of millenarian expectation and the modern world of instant Internet-delivered information have collided and fused in ways that have fanned the flames of apocalypticism and conspiracism. As the industrial and technological revolutions transformed the globe over the past two centuries, predictions of doom and disaster increased, not declined. Science did not extinguish religion but

Figure 6.2. New York City's apocalyptic end in *Amazing Stories*, January 1929. (Collection of the authors.)

developed a complex relationship with it. The two continue to merge and separate, fight and reconcile; science is the new religion, religion has become a science. The result is increased levels of both anxiety and skepticism. Hardly had the decades-long threat of nuclear winter abated when new anxieties emerged: global terrorism was given a haunting visual symbol in the twin towers of 9/11; global warming confounded millions by becoming climate change, by exhibiting a confusingly inconsistent impact on the weather, and by being denied and debated even while wildfires, hurricanes, and floods wreaked havoc and misery; meanwhile, Y2K's failure to bring catastrophe was, ironically, as alarming as it was a relief, as it seemed as if the end had merely been postponed by a dozen years.

In a way, Doomsday predictions have become the shouts of the shepherd boy who keeps crying "Wolf!" Most villagers ignore or laugh at his warnings. But, unlike in the story, there are always a few to point out that wolves really exist—and that, in the end, they get the sheep. It is often assumed that, because apocalyptic anxiety focuses on a specific date, the date *is* the phenomenon; and, thus, once the date passes—uneventfully—the fuss is over (millennialism expert Richard Landes was introduced by a colleague in 2001 as a scholar "who has nothing to do for the next 999 years"). But believers instinctively understand that—in Landes's words—"disappointment represents a critical stage in the apocalyptic process, not its dissolution."

That fact is crucial to understanding why the endless series of Doomsday false alarms that stretch back many centuries before 2012 did nothing to curtail millenarian thinking. From medieval times through the early modern centuries (roughly fifteenth through eighteenth), millenarianism prospered. Examples are far too many to detail, so we shall jump to the cluster of prophecies and predictions of the 1820s to the 1870s, and then to that of the 1970s to 2012.

Millenarianism received a new shot of energy from Protestantism, starting with the religious revolution led by Martin Luther and others in northern Europe in the sixteenth century and spreading quickly to England and Scotland. Protestant cults embracing apocalyptic thinking with fiery zeal—from Anabaptists, Calvinists, and Puritans, to Diggers, Levellers, and Ranters—flourished in the seventeenth century, first in the British Isles and the Netherlands, and then in their North American colonies. The ideological line from early New England to a Vermont farmer named William Miller, who in 1822 began proclaiming that Christ's return was imminent, is not a simple one—the history of religion in Anglo-America is complex and well-studied—but it is fair to say that it is direct.

At first, nobody listened to Farmer Miller. But then his pamphlets slowly started to sell. Millerism acquired followers in other parts of the United States, then Britain and Australia. A series of end-of-world dates were chosen in 1843 and 1844, culminating on October 22. On the day of doom, thousands climbed hills or onto rooftops—some had sold all their worldly goods—and waited to be taken up to heaven. The day became known as the Great Disappointment. The anticlimax was too much to bear for some; in a sobering anticipation of the violent denouement of later millenarian cults, there was a rash of suicides. Yet the Millerite movement survived and gave birth to several new Protestant denominations, most notably the Seventh-day Adventist Church.

Millerism was merely one of the more dramatic manifestations of millenarianism in the half-century from the 1820s to 1870s. The whole English-speaking world was affected, and other parts of Europe and the Americas too (as we saw with the Cult of the Talking Cross in the previous chapter), but the most fertile ground was the United States. Some cults were utopian and as political as they were religious—the Inspirationalists in Iowa, the Owenites in Indiana, and the Shakers in New England and New York State.

Others contributed to the development of a sort of populist, antiestablishment academia; the heirs to that tradition were 2012ologists such as Argüelles, who saw professors as jealously guarding the portals of our domain (he himself had an art history PhD and taught at various universities but was denied tenure), and Jenkins, who insisted that we run a "cliquish," "closed shop" in which "in-house scholars" cannot say "progressive things without fear of being fired." As much as 150 years ago, the modern academy was in its infancy, so the lines dividing those who were "in" (university professors) and "out" (others) were still blurred. Nevertheless, the threads of Gnosticism and millenarianism can be clearly seen in late nineteenth-century scientific and pseudoscientific investigations into astronomy and astrology, electromagnetism and clairvoyance, and ancient Egypt and pyramidology.

Anthony Aveni noted that the spirit of medieval Gnosticism was present in 2012ology—and indeed one of the most energetic 2012 encyclopedists and marketers, an Englishman named Geoff Stray, named his website 2012: Dire Gnosis. Central to Gnosticism, then and now, is both the belief in the magic of numbers—calculations and calendrics, formulas and codes—and the insistence that a mysterious, ancient, but crucial wisdom lies waiting to be uncovered.

Leaping ahead a century from Millerism, the Doomsday prophets were still at it, with 1975 being "pivotal" (as Jenkins put it) in 2012ology. Pyramidology resurfaced, but this time the focus was less on Egypt and more on Mexico and the Maya; books such as *Mexico Mystique* and the *Mysteries of the Mexican Pyramids* revealed hidden myths and meanings. This was the moment when the children of the 1960s first started using (more often, abusing) Maya calendrics, thereby laying the foundations for 2012ology. Postsixties counterculture appropriated the essence of older millenarian ideas; various imminent end-of-world dates were debated and proclaimed, until 2012 and the Maya mystique proved irresistible.

It was not only counterculture figures like Argüelles and Terence McKenna who embraced the new millenarianism. In the 1970s and 1980s, prophecy paperbacks by the hundreds sold millions of copies, feeding "an apparently insatiable market." By some accounts, no topic moved as many books as novels and nonfiction works popularizing end-time prophecy. Doomsday was on the airwaves too. In 1976, Pat Robertson predicted the world would end in 1982; in 1980, he repeated the prediction as "a guarantee" on his *700 Club* television show. Jerry Falwell (1933–2007) told television audiences for decades that the Second Coming was almost upon us. Jack Van Impe (1931–2020), a fellow broadcast evangelist, was more specific: the end was to come in Y2K; then it was to come before or in 2012; and through his final television broadcast at the end of 2019, he was interpreting and predicting world news as being full of signs that the Second Coming was imminent. Predictions that the world would end on specific dates during the 1980s and 1990s were made by a stream of published authors and preachers, among them: Willie Day Smith, a Texan radio preacher; Chuck Smith, founder of the Calvary Chapel; and Branch Davidian leader David Koresh. When Edgar Whisenant's pamphlet *88 Reasons Why the Rapture Will Be in 1988* proved to be a disappointment, he quickly published a sequel, *The Final Shout: Rapture Report 1989*. He tried again the 1990s, with each book's title updated accordingly.

It would be easy to dismiss all these prophets as kooks and criminals, and indeed some have gone to jail. For example, Rollen Stewart, famous for holding up "John 3:16" signs at sporting events, is now serving a life sentence for kidnapping, and Lee Jam Ring, founder of the Tami Church cult movement, was convicted of fraud. But the broadcasters find substantial audiences (the *700 Club*, launched in 1966, is still on the air in the 2020s), the book sales add up to the multimillions (*88 Reasons* alone sold more than two million copies), and, like the Millerites in 1844, people are regularly convinced to sell their worldly goods and follow leaders to hilltops or (with the case of Elizabeth Clare Prophet in 1990) to a Montana ranch to await the end. The result can be tragic; thirty-nine members of the Heaven's Gate cult committed suicide in a house in San Diego in 1997, convinced by their apocalyptic leader, Marshall Applewhite, that it was the only way their souls could transport up to a waiting spaceship.

It was inevitable that various forms of millenarian hysteria would bubble to the surface in 1999; that Y2K panic focused on computer crashes was a sign and symbol of the difficult relationship between old traditions of Apocalypse and new cultures of technology. That tension surfaced again after Y2K in various ways.

One fascinating example is the brief, global media blitz produced in 2003 by the discovery of a couple of scraps of paper written by Isaac Newton around 1705. Both documents contained his calculations, based on his study of the Book of Revelation, which predicted that the world would end on or after 2060. How could one of the founding fathers of modern science, asked scandalized reporters, embrace apocalyptic prophecy? Then in 2008, when scientists in Switzerland switched on the new $8 billion supercollider, some feared it would spawn a black hole that would swallow up earth. Newton is condemned, because he was a scientist, for taking the Apocalypse seriously; but science itself is feared as the possible instrument of doom. The supercollider symbolizes how far the application of scientific principles, rather than blind faith, have taken—and might take—us. But the fears it provoked remind us of that other thread—Millerism, fear of a Martian invasion, 2012 hysteria—that still runs strong in our civilization.

∽

How do the Maya fit into all this? Specifically, why has the notion that we can learn from ancient Maya wisdom had such popular appeal? The reasons are many, but we suggest four.

First of all, the popular perception of the Maya as mysterious is deeply rooted in our culture, going back at least as far as the 1840s, when John Lloyd Stephens's and Frederick Catherwood's travelogues and etchings of Maya cities uncovered by their intrepid expeditions into the jungle were best-sellers (figure 6.3 is an example; a "broken idol" at Copán). Since then, Maya studies has blossomed into a serious discipline, a major source of tourist revenue in four nations, a reference point for every genre of movie and book imaginable. In other words, the ancient Maya are an international industry, one whose beating heart is the idea that Maya civilization is a source of bottomless mystery and revelation. In short, mining the Maya for proof that 2012ology was based on something very "real" is to draw on a long tradition of Mayanist imagination.

The New Age branch of 2012ologists claimed that they had extracted "secret wisdom from lost civilizations" (in Aveni's words). The Maya have not been the sole such source, just the latest and greatest. The ancient Egyptians and the Incas have periodically received this kind of attention since the nineteenth century (as mentioned above)—Egypt experienced a massive spike in popularity in the years following the discovery of Tutankhamen's tomb in 1922, with King Tut's Curse a popular topic ever since; recent examples of modern Gnostic exposés carry titles such as *The Egypt Code* and *The Secret of the Incas*. The borderless, international purview of modern Gnosticism, combined with Western academia's "neocolonial" determination to discover and recover ancient places and peoples, has allowed us—the modern West—to claim Stonehenge, Giza, Tikal, Machu Picchu, and those who built them. For various reasons—foremost among them the recent boom in Mayanist epigraphy and archaeology—that gaze of appreciation and appropriation is fixated for now on the Maya.

The second reason why Maya Doomsday prophecy has had such modern appeal is—somewhat paradoxically—its seemingly scientific dimension. The description of Maya knowledge as based on astronomy and complex mathematics makes it seem scientific, and thus, in a way, modern. Prophetic numerology and the belief in secret codes—embedded in the Bible, in world events, in computers, even in UPC codes—has been elemental to millenarian thinking since the Middle Ages.

Figure 6.3. Frederick Catherwood, *Broken Idol at Copán*, from *Views of Ancient Monuments in Central America, Chiapas, and Yucatan*, London, 1844, tinted lithograph. (Image in the public domain.)

Whether such codes are imagined as revealing the Antichrist (with his trademark number of 666), the year of the Second Coming, or the date of a non-Christian end-times or cosmic event, belief in the numbers and enthusiasm for decoding them increased dramatically in the twentieth century—and shows no sign of abating. In a world where science is often pitted against Christianity (think evolutionism vs. creationism), the lack of a Christian context to ancient texts such as the Tortuguero monument adds to the paradoxically modern aura of Maya wisdom. One cannot help being awed by the beautiful precision of a carved date like that of Cobá's Stela 1, seeming to calculate the age of the universe so many centuries before modern physicists were able to make a similar estimate. The impression given by such calculations is that the ancient Maya were accomplished scientists a millennium or two before the West's scientific revolution even began.

A third—and closely related—explanation is the connection between the Maya calendar and astronomy. We have already discussed earlier the possibility that the Maya knew of the precession and debunked the idea that they could have known with any precision at all when it would occur—let alone predicted that the earth, sun, and the Milky Way would align in 2012. As Aveni concludes (and he has examined the topic in great detail), "It is likely that the Maya knew that what we call 'precession' existed, but to date there is no evidence to support the case that they calculated the cycle, much less even perceived precession as a cyclic phenomenon." Even if it were possible for the Maya to know this—and it is not possible—there was no such alignment taking place specifically in 2012, let alone on December 21. The alignment—that is, "the sun at winter solstice crossing the plane of the Milky Way Galaxy"—will occur during this century or the next, or perhaps the one after that. And when it does, there is no evidence at all that it will have an impact on Earth. That, of course, did not stop numerous 2012 prophets from predicting a wide array of events that would result, from global destruction to a mass spiritual awakening; nor will it stop similar predictions from periodically surfacing throughout this century (especially as casual statements by astronomers that the precession will occur "about" AD 2100 have already started to be read by some as a prediction for that very year).

More to the point here, such predictions are part of a larger phenomenon of astronomical millenarianism. These range from the relatively sober, such as anxiety over sunspots, to the hysterical, such as the Planet X theory. Every eleven years dark spots appear on the surface of the sun, caused by plasma eruptions. These eruptions produce magnetic fields and solar storms; but at worst they damage or disrupt satellites and at best they cause stunningly beautiful auroras. The sunspot cycle was predicted as peaking in 2012—ominously, some claimed, citing this as further evidence of a major cosmic occurrence. In fact, the peak passed in 2011, and sunspot activity was modest (it was heavier in 2000, as well as in the two peaks before that), and the current cycle, peaking in the early 2020s, is proving to be equally modest. Nor do such peaks climax on a specific day or even month, and there is no reason to believe that its miniscule impact on us will be any different from all the previous eleven-year peaks.

The Planet X theory claims that the ancient Sumerians predicted that a planet called Nibiru (also known as X) would collide with Earth in 2012. Needless to say, there was no such Sumerian prediction, there is no such planet, and no collision occurred. On the other hand, there are asteroids and comets moving through space, and some have hit us. This simple fact fueled fears that—Nibiru aside—an asteroid would strike Earth in 2012, or in any year in the near future, and wipe us all out, just as the massive impact of an asteroid sixty-five million years ago appears to have wiped out the dinosaurs.

This last speculation takes us back to—you guessed it—the Maya. The impact point of the asteroid that brought a dramatic Doomsday to the dinosaurs and countless other species of flora and fauna is called the Chicxulub Crater, because the massive asteroid chunk called the Baptistina fragment hit the northern Yucatan Peninsula right where the Maya fishing village of Chicxulub would later stand. Of course, the time span between the asteroid impact and the formation of Maya settlements in Yucatan was—well, about sixty-five million years (hence the event's frequent depiction as the dinosaur apocalypse; see figure 6.4). And by then the crater was buried deep underground and under the Gulf of Mexico, invisible and unknown to us until oil company geophysicists discovered it in 1978. But to some the coincidence is no coincidence at all (for those who believe, the world is full of conspiracies and codes, disguised behind apparent coincidences); surely, it was asserted, the Maya knew when the next global apocalypse would come from the sky, because they lived on top of the place where the last one happened.

Figure 6.4. Chicxulub, Yucatan, as ground zero for the dinosaur apocalypse. ("Tyrannosaurus rex and Pteranodon looking at meteorite impact in Yucatan, Mexico," Elena Duvernay/Shutterstock.com)

The fourth explanation we suggest for why the Maya seem to make such good prophets of doom is part of a larger point about how we see the Apocalypse—literally, *see* it. To be sure, depictions of Apocalypse over the centuries have been multifaceted, containing many textual and oral dimensions (as discussed earlier). But we contend, above all, that the end of the world has been conceived and perceived in visual terms. In the West, that visual dimension runs from medieval depictions of doom and the grim etchings of Dürer to the man with the sandwich board proclaiming "The End Is Nigh," and the crumbling cities depicted in magazines and movies (figures 6.2 and 6.5).

Scholars of medieval Europe have argued that the concept of the Apocalypse became so powerful because of "its dramatically symbolic mode of communication"; the final struggle between good and evil is conveyed through a wide range of symbolic opposites—such as the Four Horsemen versus the Seven Angels—that are easy to grasp and boggle the mind. These symbols were also highly visual and increasingly

Figure 6.5. Promotional postcard for *2012*, Sony Pictures, 2009. (Reproduced with permission.)

Figure 6.6. *The Apocalypse*, from "The Abingdon Apocalypse," thirteenth century, British Library, Add MS, 42555. (Image in the public domain.)

so in the late medieval and early modern centuries, as illustrated by the images in the previous three chapters. Another example is figure 6.6, a thirteenth-century Anglo-Norman depiction of the Apocalypse drawn to accompany excerpts from the Book of Revelation. The image of tumbling city buildings as a symbol of the civilized life, the world we have built, destroyed in an instant, is powerful because of its immediate visual impact. Our point is not that there is a direct line of influence from medieval manuscripts (figure 6.6) to early pulp magazines (figure 6.2) to Hollywood (figure 6.5) (although there is a larger point implied regarding the persistence of apocalyptic notions in the West), but rather that in our civilization the end of the world has for many centuries been something we *see*.

The visual nature of Maya prophecies is vivid and obvious. Even the ancient Maya texts that contribute to the myth of 2012 predictions take the form of visually impressive hieroglyphs. For centuries nobody could read these glyphs, and even today they are legible only to a small (albeit growing) number of Mayanist epigraphers. Furthermore, as we saw earlier, the translated texts remain esoteric, their apocalyptic meanings obscure and dependent upon lengthy and imaginative explanations. As a result, their larger impact is as image, not word—it is visual rather than textual. Those who have insisted on the Maya origins and foundations of 2012 draw attention to memorable motifs, not phrases—carved glyphic dates, the layout of spectacular monumental buildings, a galactic map in the form of a tree, bird, alligator, and warrior—and they are quick to appropriate visual imagery from other places, such as the Aztec Calendar Stone. Maya (or Aztec) sources shored up 2012ology not because of what they say but because of what they seem to show.

∼

What if the ancient Maya were not as good at astrology and calendrical mathematics as we think they were? What if we are not as good at interpreting Maya knowledge as we think we are? What if, in other words, the huge anticlimax of December 21, 2012, was just one in a long series of Great Disappointment dates, lulling us into a false sense of security—until the world suddenly comes to an end, without warning, on another day?

This is certainly what many believe, and there is no shortage of alternative dates. Even as Mayanists were trying to reassure the anxious in the years before 2012 that the Maya had made no such prediction, earlier dates were touted: a church group in Oakland, California, for example, distributed pamphlets in much of the United States in 2010 warning that the world would end on May 21, 2011; Carl-Johann Calleman, a contributor to the New Age branch of 2012ology whose book on the Maya calendar titled *Solving the Greatest Mystery of Our Time*, insisted that 2012 was a misreading and that on October 21, 2011, we would all have had the opportunity to enter the Universal Underworld of Consciousness.

Other predictions followed during the 2010s and into the 2020s; some are almost upon us, as we write, and hopefully will have passed uneventfully by the time you are reading these words. Predictably (as it were), the Maya have fallen somewhat out of favor, but the Aztec Calendar Stone—ironically exposed to larger audiences than ever before,

Figure 6.7. Timo Essner, "The End Is Nigh," 2020. (Reproduced with permission.)

due to its misappropriation by 2012ologists, cartoonists, and T-shirt sellers—is still being taken as a guide to the cycle that ends with the Apocalypse. One such interpretation claimed that a Zapotec prophecy, possibly inscribed on a bone, was needed to decode the Calendar Stone's warning that the end was coming in September 2017. Another—which seems to teeter on the fence between absurdity and outright parody—claims that by adapting the stone's design so it can be placed on a compact disc, one can play the CD backward and hear plans for an invasion of the earth by Reticulan aliens on July 8, 2022. The twenty-first-century decline in CD sales has surely reduced the likelihood that people will hear that warning.

Meanwhile, the millenarianism of the Middle Ages remains a cultural reference point that runs so deep it can still be parodied (see figure 6.7; one imagines a ghostly third friar saying, "Brother, I've been in the game since Y1K!"). For it doesn't matter whether the year is 2022, 2060, or 2100, whether the source is Aztec or Zapotec, a medieval monk or Isaac Newton—or *XX Reasons Why the Rapture Will Be in 20XX* (you be the prophet). Because in the end, the phenomenon is not about 2012 or any other specific year. Nor is it about the Maya. It is about the apocalyptic impulse that lies deep within our civilization. Many positive things may have come from 2012ology, and they may likewise come from future end-date predictions—such as a greater interest in and awareness of the ancient Maya and other past civilizations, of the present-day Maya and other Indigenous peoples, or of such concepts as spiritual awakening and global harmony. For this story is far from over. Just because 2012 did not bring the end of the world does not mean it ended apocalyptic anticipation; on the contrary, it was merely a stepping-stone on the millenarian pathway that is likely to persist for another . . . well, let's say, thousand years.

Sources and Suggestions for Further Reading

INTRODUCTION

The epigrams are the final line of "Discreation," a poem by the Mexican writer and environmental activist Homero Aridjis, translation by George McWhirter in the *New York Times*, October 4, 2020, "Opinion" p. 6, and in *A Time of Angels* (City Lights, 2012); and a line from the chorus of Justin Bieber's "Beauty and a Beat," written by Max Martin, Anton Zaslavski, Savan Kotecha, and Onika Maraj, on *Believe* (Island Records, 2012).

CHAPTER 1

The first translation of the Tortuguero Monument 6 text was published by Stephen D. Houston and David Stuart, "Of Gods, Glyphs, and Kings: Divinity and Rulership among the Classic Maya," *Antiquity* 70 (1996): 289–312. There are further comments by Houston, Stuart, and others on the text at the Maya Decipherment blog (mayadecipherment.com), and Stuart summarized his reading (and 2012ology's misreading) of it in *The Order of Days: The Maya World and the Truth About 2012* (Harmony Books, 2011): 25–26 and 310–15. Meanwhile, Sven Gronemeyer and Barbara MacLeod offered a comprehensive treatment of the text in "What Could Happen in 2012: A Re-Analysis of the 13-*Bak'tun* Prophecy on Tortuguero Monument 6," in *Wayeb Notes* 34 (2010), available at https://www.wayeb.org/.

Matthew Restall and Amara Solari, *The Maya: A Very Short Introduction* (Oxford University Press, 2020) is another short book by us that parallels this one, less overlapping with it and more offering an overview of Maya civilization and history from its origins to the present. There is, however, a copious literature focusing on the precontact Maya; the following works are merely a small selection of fine studies. An excellent survey that briefly details all aspects of ancient Maya life, while also deftly summarizing the debates among Mayanists, is Stephen Houston and Takeshi Inomata, *The Classic Maya* (Cambridge University Press, 2009). On Maya cities, see Scott R. Hutson, *The Ancient Urban Maya: Neighborhoods, Inequality, and Built Form* (University Press of Florida, 2016). On the decipherment of Maya writing, we recommend Michael Coe's *Breaking the Maya Code* (Thames & Hudson, 1999 revised edition), and on the political history that the glyphs record, Simon Martin and Nikolai Grube, *Chronicle of Maya Kings and Queens* (Thames & Hudson, 2008 revised edition). On Maya art, see the various books by Mary Miller; Houston, *The Life Within: Classic Maya and the Matter of Permanence* (Yale University Press, 2014); and on art and writing, Andrea Stone and Marc Zender, *Reading Maya Art: A Hieroglyphic Guide to Ancient Maya Painting and Sculpture* (Thames & Hudson, 2011). In our opinion, the best study of the "collapse" period in Maya history is by our Penn State colleague, David Webster, *The Fall of the Ancient Maya: Solving the Mystery of the Maya Collapse* (Thames & Hudson, 2002). On the calendar, see Stuart's masterful *The Order of Days* (his comments on the octillion years and "virtuosity" of the Grand Long Count are on pp. 241, 245, and 250), and Prudence M. Rice, *Maya Calendar Origins: Monuments, Mythistory, and the Materialization of Time* (University of Texas Press, 2007).

On Copan and Quiriguá, two excellent books by leading Mayanists are William L. Fash, *Scribes, Warriors and Kings: The City of Copán and the Ancient Maya* (Thames & Hudson, 1991) and Matthew Looper, *Lightning Warrior: Maya Art and Kingship at Quiriguá* (University of Texas Press, 2003).

The John Major Jenkins quote is from his alignment2012.com website, but also see his various books, such as *The 2012 Story: The Myths, Fallacies, and Truth behind the Most Intriguing Date in History* (Tarcher/Penguin, 2009). Jenkins was not a professional academic, he railed against such scholars, and he often ignored the basic rules of evidence and argument followed by Mayanists. However, he was in a different league than other nonacademic 2012 writers; he was prolific yet wrote engagingly and often persuasively, he exhibited a profound and passionate appreciation and respect for Maya culture, and above all he was well intentioned, condemning the scaremongers and insisting that 2012 would bring positive changes. His death from cancer at the age of fifty-three, just four and a half years after the end-date that he promoted so avidly, was a tragic loss.

We suggest that readers interested in moving on to additional books about the 2012 phenomenon consider Jenkins's *The 2012 Story* for the perspectives of 2012ology, and for accessible yet scholarly explorations of the ways in which Maya calendrics and astronomy have been misunderstood, Anthony Aveni's *The End of Time: The Maya Mystery of 2012* (University Press of Colorado, 2009) and Stuart's *The Order of Days*.

Unless otherwise noted, the transcriptions and translations from the *Books of Chilam Balam* are our own, made from the original manuscripts. The Edmonson and Bricker quote is from their *Supplement Volume 3: Literatures* to the *Handbook of Middle American Indians* (University of Texas Press, 1985), p. 51; and the Edmonson quotes are from his *Heaven Born Merida and Its Destiny: The Book of Chilam Balam of Chumayel* (University of Texas Press, 1986), pp. 44 and 153. Full translations of the *Chumayel* were made by Ralph L. Roys in 1933 (University of Oklahoma Press edition, 1967), of the *Tizimin* and *Chumayel* by Munro Edmonson in the 1980s (both University of Texas Press), and most recently of the *Chumayel* by Richard Luxton (Aegean Park Press, 1995).

The quote from Landa can be found in any edition of his *Relación de las cosas de Yucatán* (e.g., Dastin, 2002, p. 115), but also see Matthew Restall, Amara Solari, John F. Chuchiak IV, and Traci Ardren, *The Friar and the Maya: Diego de Landa's Account of the Things of Yucatan* (University Press of Colorado, 2022).

CHAPTER 2

The quotes at the top of the chapter are by Dennis Overbye, "Is Doomsday Coming? Perhaps, but Not in 2012," *New York Times*, November 16, 2009 (accessed at http://www.nytimes.com/2009/11/17/science/17essay.html; and from Jenkins, The 2012 Story, p. 60).

140   Sources and Suggestions for Further Reading

The placing of the Tortuguero text in the context of Naranjo and La Corona is from Stephen Houston's comments posted on the Maya Decipherment blog (mayadecipherment.com). Stuart's "wrong" and "absolutely not" quotes are from *The Order of Days*, p. 315; his "airtight" quote from p. 192. For a more detailed discussion of the Palenque glyphs, see Linda Schele and David Freidel, *A Forest of Kings: The Untold Story of the Ancient Maya* (Morrow, 1990), especially pp. 237–61.

Stephen Jay Gould's witty little book on Y2K is *Questioning the Millennium: A Rationalist's Guide to a Precisely Arbitrary Countdown* (Harmony, 1997).

The quote by Mary Ellen Miller is from p. 8 of her *Maya Art and Architecture* (Thames & Hudson, 1999). We have inserted "with" into the "brimming" quote by Houston, from a talk by him on "The Revelry of Signs" given online January 14, 2021. The Makemson essay was published as "The Miscellaneous Dates of the Dresden Codex," in *Publications of the Vassar College Observatory* 6:4 (June 1957), it is available online. Coe's *The Maya* has been published by Thames & Hudson since 1966. Our tracking of comments on 2012 by Makemson, Coe, and others was assisted by similar summaries by Jenkins, *The 2012 Story*, pp. 56–57, and in the "2012 phenomenon" entry on Wikipedia.

The discussion on precession includes quotes by Jenkins from *The 2012 Story*, p. 215, and by Aveni from *The End of Time*, pp. 100–106. The Jenkins quotes are from his http://alignment2012.com/ website and from *The 2012 Story*, his discussion of Tortuguero on pp. 217–23. The Aveni references are taken from his essay "Apocalypse Soon?" in *Archaeology* 62:6 (2009), at https://www.archaeology.org/. The Tedlock quote is from Dennis Tedlock, *2000 Years of Mayan Literature* (University of California Press, 2010), p. 136. Our discussion of the calendar draws on Tedlock's book and on Rice's *Maya Calendar Origins* (but, again, see Stuart's *The Order of Days*).

CHAPTER 3

The quotes of speech by Nebuchadnezzar are from Daniel 2:5, 2:6, and 2:31–35; the Jesus reference to Daniel is in Matthew 24. Rebecca Moore's "Middle Ages" quote is from her essay in Catherine Wessinger, ed., *Oxford Handbook of Millennialism* (Oxford University Press, 2011),

p. 287. The quote by Fernández-Armesto is from his *1492: The Year the World Began* (HarperOne, 2009), p. 144, with the Savonarola quotes taken from the same book, p. 127. The Rule of St. Francis of Assisi is reproduced widely and easily found online. The "venerable historian" quote is by John Leddy Phelan, *The Millennial Kingdom of the Franciscans in the New World: A Study of the Writings of Gerónimo de Mendieta (1525–1604)* (University of California Press, 1956), p. 1.

There is a vast scholarly literature on early Christianity, medieval European religious history, and all things to do with the history of millenarianism in Mediterranean and Western civilization—including a hefty, dense, three-volume *Encyclopedia of Apocalypticism* (Continuum, 2000), and the excellent, thirty-five-essay *Oxford Handbook of Millennialism*. Many books attempt to be both accessible and scholarly, among them Nicholas Campion, *The Great Year: Astrology, Millenarianism, and History in the Western Tradition* (Arkana, 1994), Jonathan Kirsch, *A History of the End of the World: How the Most Controversial Book in the Bible Changed the Course of Western Civilization* (Harper San Francisco, 2006), and Richard Landes, *Heaven on Earth: The Varieties of the Millennial Experience* (Oxford University Press, 2011). A fine starting point for Franciscan history is *The Franciscan Story: St. Francis of Assisi and His Influence since the Thirteenth Century* (Athena, 2008) by Maurice Carmody, himself a member of the order.

CHAPTER 4

The quote from Cortés is our translation from his second letter; see the original Spanish in Hernán Cortés, *Cartas de Relación* (Porrúa, 1983), p. 52; for the full passage in English, see Anthony Pagden, ed., *Hernán Cortés, Letters from Mexico* (Yale University Press, 1986), pp. 85–86; and for full discussion, see Matthew Restall, *When Montezuma Met Cortés: The True Story of the Meeting That Changed History* (Ecco, 2018), pp. 15–18, 45–63, and 343–45. Our quotes from Barbara Tuchman are from *The March of Folly: From Troy to Vietnam* (Ballantine, 1984), pp. 13 and 383. The Jared Diamond quote is from *Guns, Germs, and Steel: The Fates of Human Societies* (Norton, 1997), p. 80. The excerpts from The Florentine Codex are based on the definitive translation by James Lockhart, in

We People Here: Nahuatl Accounts of the Conquest of Mexico (University of California Press, 1993), p. 116.

The recent interpretations of the Aztec Calendar Stone by Milbrath and Stuart can be found through their institutions' websites (the Florida Museum and the University of Texas, respectively).

The Vespucci quote is from Felipe Fernández-Armesto's *Amerigo: The Man Who Gave His Name to America* (Random House, 2007), p. 121. The phrases from Luke are 14:21 and 14:24. For an excellent overview of the apocalyptic nature of Mendieta's writings, see Phelan's *Millennial Kingdom*; the quotes in this chapter are from pp. 6 and 8. The quotes from the native annals are in Camilla Townsend, *Here in This Year: Seventeenth-Century Nahuatl Annals of the Tlaxcala-Puebla Valley* (Stanford, 2010), using the transcriptions and translations by Townsend and James Lockhart, pp. 69, 159, and 161.

There is an extensive literature by historians, anthropologists, and other scholars on early colonial Mexico and the Spiritual Conquest; in addition to Lockhart, Phelan, and Townsend, noteworthy contributors include Louise Burkhart, Monica Díaz, Serge Gruzinski, Max Harris, Robert Haskett, Martin Nesvig, Jeanette Peterson, Amara Solari, John F. Schwaller, William B. Taylor, Jonathan Truitt, Stephanie Wood, and Mark Z. Christensen—all of whose books are relevant, but see especially *Aztec and Maya Apocalypses: Old-World Tales of Doom in a New-World Setting* (University of Oklahoma Press, 2022), which closely complements our chapters 4 and 5. For further discussion of the arguments that we make about Moctezuma and Cortés, see Restall's *Seven Myths of the Spanish Conquest* (Oxford, 2003, updated 2021) and his *When Montezuma Met Cortés*.

CHAPTER 5

On the *Books of Chilam Balam*—the original texts, translations, and the analysis by Edmonson and others—see our comments on chapter 1's sources, as well as Christensen's *Aztec and Maya Apocalypses* and his *The Teabo Manuscript: Maya Christian Copybooks, Chilam Balam, and Native Text Production in Yucatan* (University of Texas Press, 2016). On the Mayas of the Peten and Belize in the seventeenth century, see Grant D. Jones, *The Conquest of the Last Maya Kingdom* (Stanford University Press,

1998), Elizabeth Graham, *Maya Christians and Their Churches in Sixteenth-Century Belize* (University Press of Florida, 2011), and Stuart, *The Order of Days*, pp. 1–29. The quotes from Cruzob Maya rebels are taken from Victoria Reifler Bricker, *The Indian Christ, the Indian King: The Historical Substrate of Maya Myth and Ritual* (University of Texas Press, 1981), pp. 104 and 108.

There is a fine recent body of scholarly works on colonial and nineteenth-century Yucatan, from the Spanish invasions through the Caste War. In addition to Bricker, Christensen, Jones, Knowlton, and Restall (roughly half of whose books focus on colonial Yucatan), notable contributors include Pedro Bracamonte y Sosa, John F. Chuchiak, Inga Clendinnen, Don Dumond, Rajeshwari Dutt, Samuel Edgerton, Wolfgang Gabbert, William F. Hanks, Craig A. Hanson, and Robert W. Patch (for the 1761 uprising, see his *Maya Revolt and Revolution in the Eighteenth Century* [M. E. Sharpe, 2002], pp. 126–82), Sergio Quezada, Terry Rugeley, Pete Sigal, Paul Sullivan, and Amara Solari—whose books of particular relevance here are *Maya Ideologies of the Sacred: The Transfiguration of Space in Colonial Yucatan* (University of Texas Press, 2013) and *Idolizing Mary: Maya-Catholic Icons in Yucatan, Mexico* (Penn State University Press, 2019). These authors cite a further excellent body of work published in Spanish.

CHAPTER 6

The Newton quote at the top of the chapter, and our discussion of Newton that follows, is taken from a fine essay by Stephen Snobelen formerly found at www.isaac-newton.org/newton_2060.htm. The Kirban quote is in Paul Boyer, *When Time Shall Be No More: Prophecy Belief in Modern American Culture* (Belknap Press, 1992), p. 265. David Bowie's apocalyptic-pop masterpiece "Five Years" closes *The Rise and Fall of Ziggy Stardust and the Spiders from Mars* (RCA, 1972). DuPlooy's Jungle Lodge website was www.duplooys.com/index.php, and is now https://sweetsongslodge.com. Articles on other predictions included Marcelo Gleiser, "2012: The Year the World Will Not End" (May 11, 2010) on the NPR website at http://www.npr.org/blogs/13.7/2010/03/2012_the_year_the_world_will_n.html; and a hilarious piece by Chris Wright: "Alternative Endings" (November 22,

2009), in the *Boston Globe*, available at http://www.boston.com/bostonglobe/ideas/articles/2009/11/22/alternate_endings_what_if_the_world_doesnt_end_in_2012/.

The many books of Michael Shermer are easily found at booksellers or libraries. The quote by him is taken from a review by Robert T. Carroll of Shermer's *Why People Believe Weird Things: Pseudoscience, Superstition, and Other Confusions of Our Time* (Freeman & Co., 1997), at http://www.skepdic.com/refuge/weird.html. Michael Barkun discusses "improvisational millennialism" at various points throughout *A Culture of Conspiracy: Apocalyptic Visions in Contemporary America* (University of California Press, second edition, 2013). Our quotes by Norman Cohn are from *The Pursuit of the Millennium* (Oxford University Press, revised ed., 1970), p. 281.

The history of "revitalization" movements is explored and placed in millenarian contexts by Michael E. Harkin, ed., *Reassessing Revitalization Movements* (University of Nebraska Press, 2004); his introduction was especially useful to us.

The fanzine *The End Is Nigh* was found at www.endisnigh.co.uk; now see The_End_Is_Nigh entry on Wikipedia. There are a number of studies of the 1938 Wells/Welles broadcast, a recent one being John Gosling's *Waging the War of the Worlds: A History of the 1938 Radio Broadcast and Resulting Panic* (MacFarland, 2009). Douglas Cowan has published many books and articles, but his quotes here are from his essay in the *Oxford Handbook of Millennialism*, pp. 624 and 612 (in that order). The "999 years" and "disappointment" quotes are from Landes, *Heaven on Earth*, pp. xv and 5.

Jenkins offers an engaging and witty interpretation of the origins of 2012ology—and one that is notably objective considering his personal involvement in the movement—in *The 2012 Story*, pp. 82–121; pp. 124 and 218 contain his "closed shop," etc. phrases. Stray's *2012: Dire Gnosis* website is at www.diagnosis2012.co.uk/. The "mode of communication" quote is by Bernard McGinn in Richard Emmerson and McGinn, eds., *The Apocalypse in the Middle Ages* (Cornell University Press, 1992), p. 16. The Aveni quotes on precession are in his *The End of Time*, pp. 106 and 115.

Index

007. *See* Bond, James
2012: as year of Apocalypse, 1–8, 17, 27–35, 42–43, 114–17, 128, 133; Olympic Games of, 3
2012 (movie), 9, 26, 118, 120, 130, *131*
2012ology, 2, 7–8, 12, 28, 43–44, 47, 62, 67, 103–6, 110–11, 117, 123–26, 133–35
666, 128
700 Club, The, 136, 137
9/11, 122

Abraham, 54
Actopan, 83–86, *84, 85*
Aké, 93
aliens. *See* extraterrestrials; Martians
Americans. *See* United States
Anabaptists, 122
Antichrist, 105, 116, 128
Apocalypse, the. *See* Armageddon; Christ, Second Coming of; Doomsday; fear of the Apocalypse; millenarianism; prophecy and prophets
Apocalypto (movie), 39, 91
Apocalypto (lodge package), 114
Applewhite, Marshall, 125
Archangel, 25, 103

architecture. *See* Actopan; buildings; Itzmal; pyramids; temples
Argüelles, José, 32, 43–44, 111, 123–24
Aridjis, Homero, 1
Aristotle, 62
Armageddon, 42, 56
asteroids, 118, 129
astronomy, Maya, 3, 7, 19–20, 29, 36, 41–45, 126, 128. *See also* Big Dipper; comets; galactic alignment; Milky Way; Orion's Belt
Atlantis, 115
Augustinians, 83–86, 95
Australia, 123
Aveni, Anthony, 33, 43–45, 123, 126, 128
Azcapotzalco, 77
Aztecs and Aztec culture, 6, 43, 65–67, 69–78, 81–89, 135; Calendar Stone, *3*, 41, 76, 133; creation mythology, 25; New Fire Ceremony, 73–78

Babylon, 50, 52, 54
Bacabs, 25, 36, 101–3
Balam Ahau (Bahlam Ajaw), 10
Barkun, Michael, 117

145

Belize, 13, 107, 109, 113
Bieber, Justin, 1
Bienvenida, Lorenzo de, 91–93
Big Dipper, 17, 19
birds, 17–20, *18*, 25–26, 133
Bolontiku, 10–12, 25–27, 101
Bolon Yookte'. *See* Bolontiku
bombs, 3
Bond, James, 116, 120
Bowie, David, 113
Bricker, Victoria, 27
Britain and British (people), 5, 118, 122–23
buildings: Maya, 9–10, 17, 30–31, 35–39, 93–94, 133 (*see also* pyramids); Medieval European, 65, 132, *132*
Bush, George W., 55

Caesar Augustus, 105
caiman, 19, 24–27, 50
Calakmul, 110
calendrical systems: Aztec, *3*, 69–78, 133–34; Japanese, 32; Mesoamerican, 75, 106; Western, 12, 15–16, 54–56, 59–62, 105. *See also* calendrical systems, Maya (ancient); Y2K
calendrical systems, Maya (ancient): explanation of, 12, 15–16; GMT correlation, 33, 43; Grand Long Count, 19–23, 33; Long Count, 4–5, 10–12, 15–17, 19–24, 28–37, 41–45, 75, 103, 110, 114–15, 128
Calleman, Carl-Johann, 133
Calvinists, 122
Cancún, 110–11
Canek, 108
capitalism, 117
Caribbean, 79
Caste War, 107–10
Catherwood, Frederick, *92*, 126, *127*

Cauac Sky, 20–23
CBS Radio, 118
CDs (compact discs), 134
ceiba tree, 25–26
cenote, 109
Chac, 24, 27, 36, 105
Chac Chel, 24
Chachac ceremony, 105
Chan Santa Cruz, 109
Chiapas, 10, 17, 34, 78
Chichén Itzá, 1, 2, 110
Chicxulub, 129–30
Chilam Balam, Books of, 9, 16, 25–28, 100–104; of Chumayel, 25, 100–104; of Mani, 25, 26; of Tizimin, 25, 26; of Tusik, 102
chiliasm, 6, 117
Chirac, Jacques, 55
Christ, Jesus, 6, 7, 16, 32, 44, 49, 54, 55, 60, 63, 65, 80, 102, 108; Second Coming of, 7, 55–56, 59, 66, 82–83, 87, 96–97, 102, 105–6, 117, 123–24, 128
Christianity: Catholic, 6, 7, 25, 40, 49–67, 79–88, 91–111, 117; evangelical and Protestant, 5, 66, 117, 122–23, 128; Maya and Nahua, 7, 40, 85–88, 92, 93, 98, 101–11. *See also* Christ, Jesus
Cobá, 19–20, 34, 128
codes and encoded knowledge, 5–7, 17, 45, 56, 118, 124–28
Codex Borbonicus, 74, *74*
Codex Dresden, 23–27, *24*, 36, *37*, 42, 50, 101
Codex Durán, 88, *89*
Codex Telleriano-Remensis, 70, *71*
Coe, Michael, 33, 42–43
Cohn, Norman, 117
Columbus, Christopher, 49, 79–80
Comalcalco, 10
comets, 73, 88, 129

communism, 117
Complete Idiot's Guide to 2012 (Andrews), 2
conspiracism and conspiracy theories, 3, 6, 113, 115–17, 120, 129
Copán, 2, 19–20, 126, *127*
Cortés, Hernando, 69–72, 78, 86–88, 108
COVID-19 pandemic, 5, 120
Cowan, Douglas, 166
creationism, 116, 128
creation mythology. *See* Aztecs; Maya
Cruzob and the Cult of the Talking Cross, 107, 109–10, 123

Daniel, 52–56, *53*
Dargis, Manohla, 118
David (king), 54
Da Vinci Code, The (Brown), 56
Day after Tomorrow, The (movie), 26
Diamond, Jared, 72
Díaz del Castillo, Bernal, 86–87
Diggers, 122
dinosaurs, 129, *130*
Dominicans: in the Americas, 80, 95; in Europe, 60, 80
Doomsday, 1–2, 5–7, 26, 29, 55, 66, 76, 97–98, 102, 114–29
Dresden Codex. *See* Codex Dresden
duPlooy's Jungle Lodge, 113–14
Dürer, Albrecht, 49–51, 56–59, 63–64, *64*, 96, 130; *Apocalypse with Pictures* woodcuts, *51*, *57*

earthquakes, 3, 75–76, 117
Edmonson, Munro, 27–28, 103
Egypt (ancient), 12, 123–24, 126
Emmerich, Roland, 118
End Is Nigh, The (magazine), 118, *119*, 130; (Essner cartoon), *134*
England, 59, 122. *See also* Britain and British

epidemic disease and pandemics, 5, 15, 59–60, 83, 100, 120
epigraphy. *See* hieroglyphs
eschatology, 6, 54, 56, 118
evolutionism, 128
extraterrestrials, 5, 44, 115, 118–20, 125, 134

Falwell, Jerry, 124
Family Radio, 113
famine, 15, 59–60
fear of the Apocalypse or world ending: Aztec, 74; Maya, 2–4, 39; non-Maya, 1–5, 7, 8, 50, 116–25
Fernández-Armesto, Felipe, 62
Final Judgment. *See* Last Judgment
Flood, the, and floods, 9, 17, 24–27, 36, 50, 76, 101–3, 122
Florence and Florentines, 49, 60–62, 79
Florentine Codex, 72, 87–88
Four Horsemen of the Apocalypse, 50, 130. *See also* Dürer
Franciscans: in the Americas, 7–8, 25, 65–67, 69, 78–83, 87–89, 91–109, 114; in Europe, 49–66, *64*, 79–80
frogs, 36

galactic alignment and convergence, 17–19, 33, 43–45, 128, 133. *See also* precession
Garden of Eden, 49
Gibson, Mel, 39, 91
Giza, 2, 126
global warming and extreme weather, 3, 4, 45, 76, 115, 122
Gnosticism, 43, 55–56, 111, 123–26
Gog, 54–55
Gómara, Francisco López de, 87
Good Friday, 105
Gould, Stephen Jay, 32
Granada, 87

Grand Canyon, 2
Great Disappointment, the, and apocalyptic disappointment, 60, 115, 122–25, 133
Greek, 6, 44
Guatemala, 7, 13, 20, 30, 78, 100, 107, 113

Hancock, Graham, 111
heart sacrifice, 73–75
Heaven's Gate, 125
Hellmouth, 58, *59*, *85*, 86
Henry of Bloise, 59
Hero Twins, 17–19
hieroglyphs, Maya, 9–13, *11*, 16–28, *21*, *22*, *24*, 29–45, *30*, *37*, 101, *127*, 132–33
Hipparchus, 44
Hippolytus, 55
Hollywood, 132. *See also* 007; *2012*; *Apocalypto*; *The Day after Tomorrow*
Holocaust denial, 115
Honduras, 13, 19
Houston, Stephen, 12, 31, 39
Huixachtlán, 73. *See also* Aztecs; New Fire Ceremony
humor, 39, 118, 120, 122
hurricanes, 3, 45, 76, 122
Hussein, Saddam, 54

Incas, 126
Innocent III (pope), 65
Inquisition, Spanish, 83, 98–102
Inspirationalists, 123
International Star Party, 2
Internet, the, 1–2, 5, 7, 44, 47, 120
Iraq, 54
Israel, 54
Italy, 60–65
Itzá Maya (kingdom), 107–8
Itzam Cab Ain, 26–27
Itzamnaaj, 93–94

Itzcoatl, 77
Itzmal (Izamal), 92–97, 100; Virgin of, 94, 96, 97, *97*, 108
Ix Ahau Na (Lady House), 36, *37*
Izapa, 17–19, 44–45; Stela 25, 17–19, *18*

Jenkins, John Major, 2, 17, 19, 29, 31–32, 44–45, 111, 123–24
Jerusalem and New Jerusalem, 52, 54, 59, 88–89, 102, 106
Jesuits, 95
Jimmu (emperor), 32
Joachim of Fiore, 60
Johnson, Cody, 111
Joseph, Lawrence, 45
Josephus, 88
Judaism and Jews, 5, 50–55, 80, 82
Judgement Day. *See* Doomsday

King of England, 59
King of Spain, 70, 86–87
K'inich Janaab' Pakal, 10, 35
Kirban, Salem, 113
Knowlton, Timothy, 102, 105
Koresh, David, 124
k'uhul ajaw (*kul ahau*), 10, 13, 34–39. *See also* kings and kingship; Maya
Kukulcan, 70

La Corona, 30–31
Lake Aztlan, 77
Lake Texcoco, 73, 88
Lamanai, 107
Landa, Diego de, 25, 91–94, 97–102, *99*
Landes, Richard, 122
language: German, 49; Latin, 49; Nahuatl, 66, 72, 73, 78, 81, 87–88; Spanish, 78, 85, 88, 109; Zapotec, 134–35. *See also* language, Mayan

language, Mayan, 6, 13, 15–17, 25, 39, 70, 102–3, 109; K'iche', 16, 17, 25, 70; Yucatec, 15, 16, 25, 70, 102–3, 109
Las Casas, Bartolomé de, 80
Last Judgment, 49, 57, 59, 62, 85–86, 98, 102, 117. *See also* Doomsday
Las Vegas, 117
Levellers, 122
libertarianism, 117
London, 3, 118
Long Count. *See* calendrical systems, Maya
Looper, Matthew, 20, 22
Los Angeles, 117
Lucan, 88
Luke, Book of, 80–82
Luther, Martin, 122
Lyra, Nicolas de, 79–82

Machu Picchu, 2, 126
Madrid Codex, 36
maize and corn, 17, 25, 36, 38, 73, 101, 103
Makemson, Maud, 42
Mani, 25, 26, 45, *46*, 98–99
Manifest Destiny, 117
maps, 17, *18*, 44–46, *46*, 107, 133
Martians, 118, 120, 125
Marxism, 117
Maya: ancient, 1–4, 6–47; ballcourts and ballgame, 17, 39; civilization (characteristics), 13–28, 38–41; collapse, 41; colonial-era, 91–110; creation mythology, 13, 16–28, 35–39, 45, 100–109; hieroglyphs (*see* hieroglyphs, Maya; writing); kings and kingship, 10, 13, 20–23, 34–39, 107–8; language (*see* language, Mayan); mathematics, 1, 12, 16, 19–23, 32–37, 43–44, 126, 128, 133; religion, 3, 10, 13, 15, 34, 38, 91–110. *See also* astronomy; calendrical systems; Christianity; prophecy and prophets; scribes
Mayanists, 2, 10, 15–17, 20, 27, 31–33, 35, 38, 39, 41–44, 103, 126, 133
McKennah, Terrence, 124
Mecca, 32
Medieval Europe and Middle Ages, 49–67, 69, 79–80, 86, 100, 110–11, 117–18, 122, 123, 126, 130, 132, *132*, 135
Mendieta, Gerónimo, 81–83
Merida, 27, 91–92, 97–99, 103, 105, 108, 110
Mesoamerica, 25, 34, 47, 50, 54, 66, 70, 75, 77, 82, 91, 106, 115
Metropolitan Museum of Art, 10
Mexico, 6, 9–10, 13, 15, 17, 34, 47, 59, 69–89, 100, 106–10, 124
Milbrath, Susan, 75
Milky Way, 17, 19, 44, 128
millenarianism, 6–7, 29, 37–43, 49–67, 69, 73–89, 100–110, 114–35
millennialism, 6–7, 28, 50, 55–66, 69, 80–85, 97, 100–106, 116–22
Miller, Mary Ellen, 39
Miller, William, and Millerism, 123–25
Minoans, 12
mission churches. *See* Actopan; Itzmal
Mixtecs, 66
Moctezuma, 69–78, 86–89, *89*, 108
Mongols, 54
Montana, 125
Montanus, 55
Morley Manuscript, 102
Motolinía, 87–88
Mount Verna, 63

Muhammad, 32
Muslims, 80, 82, 87

Nahuas and Nahuatl-speakers, 66, 69–89, 100. *See also* Aztecs
Naranjo, 30–31
natural disasters, 2–3, 40, 47, 83
Nebuchadnezzar, 52–54, *53*
Netherlands, the, 122
New Age, 7, 42–43, 111, 126, 133
New England, 122–23
New Jersey, 120
Newton, Sir Isaac, 113, 125, 135
New York, 10, 120, *121*, 123
New York Times, 29, 118, 120
nuclear war and weapons, 3, 5, 120, 122

Oaxaca, 78
oil, 3, 129
omens, 73, 88, *89*
Orion's Belt, 73
Owenites, 123
Oxlahuntiku, 25–27, 103

Page, Christine, 111
Pakal. *See* K'inich Janaab' Pakal
Palenque, 9–10, 34–36, 110; Temple of the Cross, 35–36, *35*
Paris, 79; Codex, 36
Phelan, John, 69
pilgrimage and pilgrims, 59–60, 65, 92–96
Pinchbeck, Graham, 111
Piraro, Dan, 2, *3*, *4*
plague. *See* epidemic disease and pandemics
planets and planetary movements. *See* astronomy
Planet X, 129
Plato, 62

Plutarch, 88
Pope Innocent III, 65
Popol Vuh (book), 16, 19, 25
precession, 44–45, 128
priests: Aztec, 73–75; Maya, 5–6, 13, 34, 39, 93, 108–9; Spanish (*see* Augustinians; Dominicans; Franciscans; Inquisition, Spanish)
Principal Bird Deity, 17, 19, 20
prophecy and prophets: Christian (non-Maya), 5, 9, *61*, 62, 80, 82, 96, 113, 124–26; Islamic, 5; Jewish, 5, 55; Maya, 5–6, 9, 12, 25, 29–31, 91, 102, 108, 130–32; modern, 6–7, 17, 33, 42, 111, 114–29, 133–35
Prophet, Elizabeth Clare, 125
Prophets Conference, the, 111
Protestantism. *See* Christianity
Puebla, 81
Puritans, 122
pyramidology, 123–24
pyramids, 2, 10, 38, 41, 73, 81, 92–94, 124

Quetzalcoatl, 69–71, 86–87
Quintana Roo, 109
Quiriguá, 20–23, 34; Stela C, 20–23, *21*, *22*

Ranters, 122
Revelation, Book of, 6, 50, 56, 60, 89, 91, 96–97, 101, 125, 132
Rice, Prudence, 20
Ring, Lee Jam, 125
Ritual of the Bacabs (book), 36
Riviera Maya, 110–11
Robertson, Pat, 124
Roman Empire, 55
Roys, Ralph, 103
Russia, 54

Index   151

sacbeob (white roads), 93
Sahagún, Bernardino de, 88
Saint Francis of Assisi. See Franciscans
Saint John, 50, 56, 82, 96, 125
Satan, 5, 56, 59, 81, 98
Savonarola, Girolamo, 49, 60–63
science and pseudo-science, 9, 17, 63, 115, 120–22, 125, 128
scientific revolution, 66, 128
Scotland, 122
scribes, Maya, 6–7, 12, 16, 19–28, 33–39, 43–45, 47, 50, 100–106, 109. See also Chilam Balam; hieroglyphs, Maya; writing
Sepúlveda, Juan Ginés de, 70
Seven Macaw, 17–19, *18*
Seventh-Day Adventist Church, 117, 123
Shakers, 123
Shermer, Michael, 115
Sicily, 60
Smith, Hubert, 91
Smith, Willie Day, 124
solar flares, 45
Spaniards, 7, 13, 45, 47, 82–88, 92, 97, 102
Spanish invasion and conquest, 13, 40, 67, 69–73, 78, 86–88, 105–10. See also Augustinians; Dominicans; Franciscans
Stephens, John Lloyd, 126
Stewart, Rollen, 125
Stonehenge, 2, 12, 126
Stray, Geoff, 31, 124
Stuart, David, 11, 12, 19–20, 30–31, 33, 75, 78
suicide, 98, 123, 125
sunspots, 129
supercollider, 125
survival kits, 2
Sweet Songs (lodge), 113–14

Switzerland, 125

Tabasco, 9–10
Talking Cross, Cult of. See Cruzob
Tanakh, 54
Tedlock, Dennis, 36
Tehuantepec, 78
temples: Aztec, 73, 81, 88; Maya, 10, 15, 34–38
Tenochtitlán, 70, 73, 88
terrorism, 3, 120, 123
Tikal, 2, 41, 113, 114, 126
Tlatelolco, 88
Tlaxcala, 81
Tortuguero, El, 9–12, *11*, 28–31; Monument 6, 10–12, 17, 27–31, 43, 128
torture, 85–86, 98, 100, 108
tourism, 1–2, 98, 110–13, 118, 126
Trojan Horse, 72
tsunamis, 3, 45. See also floods
Tuchman, Barbara, 72
Tula, 69
Tulum, 110
Turkey, 55
Tutankhamen, 126

Uc, Jacinto Canek Moctezuma, 108
UFOs, 115. See also extraterrestrials
United States and Americans (people), 5, 7, 110, 117, 120–23, 133
university (faculty and classes), 8, 55, 123
UPC codes, 126
utopia, 7, 117, 123

vacations. See tourism
Van Impe, Jack, 124
Venus, 29, 36
Vespucci, Amerigo, 69, 79

Vietnam, 72
Virgin Mary, 94–97, 108. *See also* Itzmal
Virgo, 36
volcanoes, 3, 73

War of the Worlds, The (Wells), 118, 120
Welles, Orson, 118
Wells, H. G., 118, 120
Whisenant, Edgar, 124
Winchester, Bishop of, 58–59

writing, Maya: ancient (*see* hieroglyphs, Maya); colonial-era (alphabetic), 7, 9, 13, 16, 47, 50, 100–106, 109. *See also* Chilam Balam; scribes

Y2K, 1, 19, 31–32, 115, 118, 122, 124–35
Yucatan, 7, 13, 19, 25, 36, 45, 91–111, 127–30

Zapotecs, 66, 134–35
zombies, 5

About the Authors

Matthew Restall and **Amara Solari** are specialists in Maya culture and colonial Mexican history. Between them they have over forty years of experience studying Mayan languages and researching the Maya past in the towns and archives of Mexico, Central America, and Spain. Their knowledge of Yucatec Maya gives them the rare ability to decipher the original Maya texts, glyphic and alphabetic. Both teach at the Pennsylvania State University, where Restall is Edwin Erle Sparks Professor of Latin American History and Anthropology and Solari is professor of art history and anthropology. His books include *Maya Conquistador, Seven Myths of the Spanish Conquest,* and *When Montezuma Met Cortés.* Her books include *Maya Ideologies of the Sacred* and *Idolizing Mary.* They recently coauthored *The Maya* for Oxford University Press's *Very Short Introductions* series.

www.ingramcontent.com/pod-product-compliance
Lightning Source LLC
Chambersburg PA
CBHW050732240426
43665CB00053B/2214